history at source

NAZI GERMANY *1933-1945*

John Laver

Hodder & Stoughton

A MEM

The cover illustration is a poster designed by Felix Albrecht in 1932. The caption reads: 'We farmers are mucking out. We vote List 2 National Socialist'.

Order queries: Please contact Bookpoint Ltd, 39 Milton Park, Abingdon, Oxon OX14 4TD. Telephone: (44) 01235 400414. Fax: (44) 01235 400454. Lines are open from 9 am - 6 pm Monday to Saturday, with a 24-hour message answering service. Email address: orders@bookpoint.co.uk

British Library Cataloguing in Publication Data

Lava, John
  Nazi Germany 1933-45. – (history at source).
1. Germany, history, 1933–1945
  I. Title   II. Series
  943.086

ISBN 0 340 54350–7

First published 1991
Impression number   13 12 11 10
Year   2004 2003 2002 2001 2000

Typeset by Input Typesetting Ltd, London.
Printed in Great Britain for Hodder & Stoughton Educational, a division of Hodder Headline Plc, 338, Euston Road, London NW1 3BH by Redwood Books, Trowbridge, Wiltshire.

CONTENTS

PREFACE

The history of Nazi Germany has long been a popular topic with students studying at A Level, AS Level, Higher Grade and beyond. Changes in the requirements of examination boards, involving particularly the greater use of source-based questions, coursework and personal assignments, have not decreased the popularity of the topic.

This book is intended for students, and hopefully teachers, who are interested in the topic of Nazi Germany and who would welcome a practical complement to existing textbooks and monographs. Several topics are covered by an introduction and a collection of mainly primary sources, together with questions of the type likely to be encountered in examinations, or other exercises involving the use of sources. Practical advice is proffered on the way to approach such questions, and a specimen answer is included. Guidance is also offered on the approach to essay questions. Sample essay titles are given along with suggestions on relevant approaches; and again, a specimen answer is included. Finally, a brief analytical bibliography is intended to give guidance to teachers and students alike.

It is hoped that this collection will prove useful to students working as part of an organised course or on their own.

APPROACHING SOURCE-BASED

QUESTIONS

Source-based questions have become an important part of History examinations at all levels in recent years. Students who have studied History at GCSE and Standard Grade will be used to handling various types of sources. The skills they have learned in handling evidence will continue to be applicable at a more advanced level, but there will also be more sophisticated skills to master and the sources themselves may be more demanding.

During your studies you will encounter both primary and secondary historical evidence. The distinction between the two is sometimes artificially exaggerated: all sources have their value and limitations, and it is possible to worry unnecessarily about a 'hierarchy of sources'. The important thing for the student is to feel confident in handling all sources. The majority of sources in this book are primary sources, since they are the raw material from which historians work; and they are mostly of a documentary nature, since that is the type most commonly found in examinations. However, there are also statistics and examples of visual evidence. The comments below will usually apply to *all* types of evidence.

When a student is faced with a piece of historical evidence, there are certain questions that he or she should always ask of that source; but in an examination that student will be asked specific questions set by an examiner, and, in the light of pressures, not least of which is time, it is important to approach these questions in an organised and coherent fashion. The following advice should be borne in mind when answering source-based questions. Some of the advice may appear obvious in the cold light of day, but, as examiners will testify, the obvious is often ignored in the cauldron of the examination room!

1 Read the sources carefully before attempting to answer the questions, whether there is one source or a collection of them. This will give you an overview of the sources which will usually be connected and related to a particular theme. You will study the individual sources in detail when you answer specific questions.

2 Always look carefully at the attribution of the sources: the author and date of publication; the recipient, if any; the context in which the source was produced. All these will often give you an insight in addition to that provided by the content of the source itself.

3 Mark allocations are usually given at the end of each question or sub-question. Ignore the marks at your peril! The number of marks

will almost certainly give you some indication of the length of answer expected. Length of answer is not an indicator of quality, and there is no such thing as a standard answer, but it is commonplace for candidates in examinations to write paragraph-length answers to questions carrying one or two marks. A question carrying such a low mark can usually be adequately answered in two or three sentences. You do not have the time to waste your purple prose in examinations! Similarly, a mark allocation of nine or ten marks indicates the expectation of a reasonably substantial answer.

4 Study the wording of the questions very carefully. Some questions will ask you to use *only* your own knowledge in the answer; some will ask you to use *both* your own knowledge *and* the source(s); some will insist that you confine your answer to knowledge gleaned from the source(s) *alone*. If you ignore the instructions, you will certainly deprive yourself of marks.

5 If there are several sources to be consulted, ensure that you make use of the ones to which you are directed – candidates have been known to ignore some or choose the wrong ones!

6 Certain types of question require a particular type of response:
a) Comparison and/or contrasting of sources: ensure that you do consider all the sources referred to in the question.
b) Testing the usefulness and limitations of sources: if you are asked to do both, ensure that you do consider both aspects. You may be required to evaluate a source in relation to other information provided, or in the context of your own background knowledge of the subject.
c) Testing reliability. This is not the same as considering the utility of a source, although students sometimes confuse the two concepts.
d) Phrases such as 'Comment upon', 'Analyse' or 'Assess'. Ensure that you do what is asked. Do not be afraid of quoting extracts from a source in your answer, but avoid over-quotation or too much direct paraphrasing, since questions will usually, although not always, be testing more than comprehension. You should therefore simply be illustrating or amplifying a particular point. Always *use* the sources and do not just regurgitate what is in front of you.
e) Synthesis: this is a high level skill which requires you to blend several pieces of evidence and draw general conclusions.

7 If at all possible, avoid spending too much time on the sources questions in examinations. Frequently candidates answer the sources questions thoroughly but do not allow themselves enough time to do justice to the rest of the examination paper, and essay answers sometimes suffer in consequence if they are attempted last.

8 If possible, read published examiners' reports which will give you

3

further indication as to the most useful approaches to particular questions, and the pitfalls to avoid.

A Note on this Collection of Sources

It is the intention of this collection to give ideas to teachers and realistic examples of sources and questions to students, either for use in schools and colleges or for self-study purposes. However, they are intended to be flexible. If it is found helpful, adapt the questions or mark allocations, or devise new questions; or use the sources as part of coursework or personal studies. You might even find it an interesting exercise to put together your own sources and appropriate questions.

1 THE NAZI RISE TO POWER

The Weimar Republic enjoyed a brief life of only fourteen years before Hitler's appointment as Chancellor in January 1933 and the subsequent establishment of the Third Reich. The Republic, born in the aftermath of defeat in the First World War and suffering the humiliation of having to sign the hated Treaty of Versailles, inspired no widespread enthusiasm, despite a period of relative prosperity in the late 1920s. The onset of the Great Depression enabled opposing parties of the Left and Right, particularly the Nazis and the Communists, to exploit fears and resentments latent since the end of the War. The economic crisis enabled the Nazis, in particular, to develop into a mass party with considerable popular support. Hitler managed to present the image of a dynamic, thrusting party, which was able to appeal to different elements in German society – the young, those with nationalist fervour or racial prejudice, anti-Communists, small businessmen and farmers. The party could also play upon the fears of Conservatives and big businessmen who disliked both Weimar democracy and the perceived threat of a Marxist Revolution.

By 1932 the Nazis formed the largest party in the Reichstag. The Party itself was rapidly expanding, and contained sometimes contradictory interests, making it not an easy organisation to control. Hitler, however, had the confidence to hold out for the position of Chancellor through the setback of the election of November 1932 when the Nazi surge faltered, and some of his supporters were urging a compromise deal with the right-wing establishment. The dilemma of how to achieve ultimate power was resolved by the offer of the Chancellorship in January 1933.

Hitler's attempt to seize power by force in 1923 had failed. Thereafter he had worked through the constitution he detested whilst his SA created disorder in the streets. Although Hitler never received the electoral support of the majority of the German people, he did generate enough mass support at a time of political and economic crisis to persuade the right-wing establishment to persuade the aged President Hindenburg to appoint him as Chancellor, in the mistaken belief that Hitler could be controlled in the interests of others.

A Motives for joining the Nazi Party

(i) I observed many things in Berlin which could not be noticed – or only to a lesser degree – in small towns. I saw the Communist danger, the Communist terror, their gangs breaking up 'bourgeois' meetings, the 'bourgeois' parties being utterly helpless, the Nazis being the only party that broke terror by anti-terror. I saw the complete failure of the 'bourgeois' parties to deal with the economic crisis. . . Only national socialism offered any hope. Anti-semitism had another aspect in Berlin: Nazis mostly did not hate Jews individually, many had Jewish friends, but they were concerned about the Jewish problem. . . Nobody knew of any way to deal with it, but they hoped the Nazis would know. If they had guessed how the Nazis did deal with it, not one in a hundred would have joined the party.

From a letter by the Headmaster of Northeim's Girls' High School, 1967, in W. Allen: *The Nazi Seizure of Power* (1984)

(ii) It was the depression and business was bad. The Nazis used to ask my father for contributions and he refused. As a consequence of this he lost business. So he joined the Nazi Party. But this lost him other customers, so he was discouraged by the whole situation. He probably wouldn't have joined of his own choice.

By the Owner of a printing shop in Northeim, in W. Allen: *The Nazi Seizure of Power* (1984)

B Social Composition of the Nazi Party in 1930

Occupational category	Nazi Party %	German society %	Index (German soc = 100)
Workers	28.1	45.9	61.2
White-collar workers	25.6	12.0	213.5
Self-employed	20.7	9.0	230.0
Civil servants	6.6	4.2	157.1
Teachers	1.7	0.9	188.8
Peasants	14.0	10.6	132.0
Others	3.3	17.4	18.9
	100	100	

Compiled from various German statistics

C Hitler Woos the Industrialists
It is natural that if the able minds of a nation, who are always in a minority, are given an equal valuation with all the rest, the final result will inevitably be an outvoting of genius, an outvoting of ability and personal worth, an outvoting which is then falsely described as the rule of the people. For that is not the rule of the people, but in reality the rule of stupidity, of mediocrity, of incompleteness, of

cowardice, of weakness, of inadequacy. People's rule is rather to have a people governed and led in all spheres of life by those individuals who are most capable and therefore born to rule than to let every sphere of life be administered by a majority which is naturally and inevitably unfamiliar with the sphere of life concerned.

Thus democracy will lead in practice to the destruction of the true values of a people.

From a speech made by Hitler to the 'Industry Club' at Düsseldorf, 27 January 1932

D Sequel to the Election of 6 November 1932
Allow me to express my special congratulations on the firm attitude which you adopted immediately after the elections. There exists in my mind no doubt that the development of events can only have one end and that is your chancellorship. It looks as if our attempt to obtain a row of signatures in favour of it from economic life will not be entirely fruitless, although I am inclined to think that heavy industry will hardly join in, for it really justifies its name 'heavy industry' by its ponderousness.

I hope that in the coming days and weeks the small unevennesses which necessarily creep into propaganda will not be so marked as to give opponents an opportunity for justifiable indignation. The stronger your position intrinsically, the more gentlemanly the form of struggle can be. The more events go your way, the more you can afford to dispense with attacks on personalities.

I am filled with optimism because the whole present system is certainly dying of exhaustion.

With German greeting,
Yours very sincerely,
Dr. Hjalmar Schacht

From a letter by Schacht, Ex-President of the Reichsbank, to Hitler, 12 November 1932

E The Eve of Power
8 December 1932
The Inspectors of the Party are gathered at the Führer's. All are in a very depressed mood. . .

The Führer walks up and down with long strides in his hotel room hour after hour. His features show that his mind is powerfully at work. . . Once he stops and says only: 'If the Party breaks up, I will finish myself off in three minutes with a pistol.'

5 January 1933
The discussion between the Führer and Herr von Papen in Cologne

has taken place. It was supposed to be kept secret, but, through an indiscretion, has become publicly known and Schleicher is now having it trumpeted up in a big way in the press. . . One thing the government now in office must know is that its overthrow is seriously on the cards. If this coup succeeds, then we are no longer far removed from power.

Excerpts from the *Goebbels Diaries* (1934)

F The Reaction of the Left
The bloody, barbarous terror-regime of fascism is being set up in Germany. Masses, do not allow the deadly enemies of the German people, the deadly enemies of the workers and poor peasants, of the working people in town and country, to carry out their crime! . . .
   Out on the streets!
   Bring the factories to a halt!
   Reply at once to the onslaught of the fascist bloodhounds with strikes, with mass strikes, with the general strike!

From a Communist Party leaflet of 30 January 1933

Questions

1 a What information can be gleaned from Source B about the composition of the Nazi Party in the years immediately before its accession to power? **(5 marks)**
   b How do you account for this composition? **(5 marks)**

2 What motives for supporting the Nazi Party can be deduced from Sources A and B? **(6 marks)**

3 What do Sources C and D suggest about Hitler's political skills? **(6 marks)**

4 Using your own knowledge, explain the reference to Hitler's 'firm attitude' described in Source D. **(3 marks)**

5 Using your own knowledge, explain the change in Goebbels' and Hitler's attitude between the dates of the two extracts, as revealed in Source E. **(5 marks)**

6 a Account for the tone of Source F. **(4 marks)**
   b How useful is Source F to an historian investigating Hitler's accession to power? **(4 marks)**

7 To what extent do Sources A–F prove the assertion that Hitler came to power by backstairs intrigue rather than popular support? **(10 marks)**

2 THE CONSOLIDATION OF POWER
1933–4

Hitler's appointment to the Chancellorship in January 1933 was only the prelude to the period known as '*Gleichschaltung*' or 'Co-ordination', during which most institutions in Germany were brought, to a greater or lesser extent, under Nazi control. Although Hitler did not yet possess supreme power – the Presidency and the Army, for example, remained independent institutions – in the months after January most institutions which might have harboured opposition to the Nazis were undermined. The Reichstag fire was used to whip up anti-Communist fears and the Enabling Law gave Hitler extraordinary powers. The state governments were subordinated to Berlin; the trade unions were dissolved and replaced by a Nazi organisation, the Nazi Labour Front; the Nazi Party became the only legal party in Germany; even the Catholic Church was compromised into signing a concordat with the Government. The civil service was purged and Nazi ideas were insinuated into schools and universities. Furthermore, cultural activities were taken under Nazi control.

The reasons for the relative ease with which the Nazis achieved 'co-ordination' have been vehemently debated. The institutionalisation of terror, signified by the arrest of real or potential opponents, and the establishment of concentration camps were certainly important factors; as was the insinuation of Nazi propaganda into all aspects of life. Certainly dedicated opponents of the Nazis faced enormous problems when attempting to focus their discontent. Yet it was also the case that Hitler achieved much popular support through the dynamic urgency of his patriotic slogans and apparent determination to 'get things done'. The millions of votes Hitler received in the March 1933 election were certainly not all achieved through intimidation. Another factor in the equation was the fact that the Nazis began to reap the benefits of an economic recovery already under way before they came to power.

For all his success at 'co-ordination', Hitler faced problems from within his own movement. The latent contradictions and conflicting interest groups within the Nazi movement surfaced after the 'First Revolution' of January 1933. The SA leaders, for example, expected to share the fruits of power and replace the professional German army with a revolutionary people's militia. Nazis like Gregor Strasser, who took the Socialist elements of the Nazi programme more seriously than Hitler, were seen as a threat by the industrialists financing Hitler; and many Nazi leaders had their own corners to fight and scores to settle as they vied for positions of power under Hitler.

However, demands for a 'Second Revolution', a genuine transformation of Germany into a radical society protected by a people's army, could not be tolerated by Hitler, whose increasing preoccupation was to expand the existing army. Any doubts Hitler may have had were resolved by a pact with the Generals; by the promptings of his own lieutenants, afraid of the SA (which had never been fully integrated into the Nazi Party); and by the awareness that conservative opposition also existed, as suggested in Vice-Chancellor von Papen's speech at Marburg.

On the Night of the Long Knives (30 June 1934) the SA leadership and enemies of the regime, real or imagined, were bloodily removed. This step, along with Hitler's absorption of the Presidency on Hindenburg's death (1 August), effectively meant that military expansion and order were to be the idols of the new Nazi State. There would be no radical social and political transformation of Germany in the way that some of the more naive Nazi supporters had hoped.

A The New Chancellor Appeals to the German People

... It is an appalling inheritance which we are taking over. The task before us is the most difficult which has faced German statesmen in living memory. But we all have unbounded confidence, for we believe in our nation and in its eternal values. Farmers, workers, and the middle class must unite to contribute the bricks wherewith to build the new Reich.

The National Government will therefore regard it as its first and supreme task to restore to the German people unity of mind and will. It will preserve and defend the foundations on which the strength of our nation rests. It will take under its firm protection Christianity as the basis of our morality, and the family as the nucleus of our nation and our state. Standing above estates and classes, it will bring back to our people the consciousness of its racial and political unity and the obligations arising therefrom. It wishes to base the education of German youth on respect for our great past and pride in our old traditions. It will therefore declare merciless war on spiritual, political and cultural nihilism. Germany must not and will not sink into Communist anarchy. . .

Now, German people, give us four years and then judge us. . .

From Hitler's 'Appeal to the German People', 31 January 1933

B A Nazi Election Appeal

Residents of Northeim!
You want to continue your work in peace and quiet! You've had enough of the impudent behaviour of the SPD and the KPD! You want the red Senators, Councilmen, and Reichsbanner Generals with

all their armed followers to go to the Devil! . . . In the barracks were brutalised Communists, armed with military rifles . . . waiting for the bloody work in the streets of Northeim. . . The NSDAP, the SA, the SS are fighting for you, even here in Northeim! Tomorrow is the day of the awakened nation! At the ballot boxes the German *Volk* thanks the great Führer for its salvation in the last hour! A storm will sweep through Germany! Germany Votes List 1! *Heil Hitler*!

Appeal by NSDAP, Local Group Northeim, 3 and 4 March 1933, quoted in W. Allen, *The Nazi Seizure of Power* (1984)

C Hitler Addresses German Industrialists

. . . Private enterprise cannot be maintained in the age of democracy; it is conceivable only if the people have a sound idea of authority and personality. . . I recognised . . . that new ideas must be sought conducive to reconstruction. I found them in Nationalism, in the value of personality, in the denial of reconciliation between nations, in the strength and power of individual personality. . .

Now we are facing the last election. No matter what the outcome, there will be no retreat, even if the coming election does not bring about a decision. . . There will, however, be no internal peace until Marxism is eliminated.

From a speech by Hitler to about twenty industrialists, 20 February 1933

D A Purge of the Civil Service

Officials who are of non-aryan descent are to be placed in retirement. . .

Officials whose past political activity does not furnish a guarantee that they will at all times identify themselves unreservedly with the national state may be dismissed the service. . .

From the 'Law for the Restoration of the Professional Civil Service', 7 April 1933

E The Destruction of the Trade Unions

The Government of the National Revolution has raised the 1st of May to the status of Festival Day of the Nation's Labour. . . For the first time after decades of inner cleavage and disruptive party conflict, the immortal spirit of German folkdom is raising itself again above wrangling and discord. . .

Marxism lies in ruins. The organisations of class conflict are shattered.

From a proclamation by Goebbels, Minister of Public Enlightenment and Propaganda, 24 April 1933

F The Abolition of the Parliamentary System

The sole political party in Germany is the National Socialist German Workers' Party.

Whoever attempts to maintain the organised existence of another political party, or to form a new political party, shall . . . be punished with hard labour of up to three years or with imprisonment of from six months to three years' duration.

From the 'Law Against the Revival of Old or the Formation of New Parties', 14 July 1933

G Conflict Within the Nazi Movement

A tremendous victory has been won. But not absolute victory! . . .

In the new Germany the disciplined brown storm battalions of the German revolution stand side by side with the armed forces. . .

The SA and SS are the foundation pillars of the coming National Socialist State – their State for which they have fought and which they will defend. . . The SA and SS will not tolerate the German revolution going to sleep or being betrayed at the half-way stage by non-combatants . . . the brown army is the last levy of the nation, the last bastion against Communism. . .

From a newspaper article by Ernst Röhm, June 1933

H Hitler Justifies the 1934 Purge

. . . Chief of Staff Röhm entered into relations with General Schleicher through an utterly corrupt and dishonest go-between. . . General Schleicher . . . spelt out the secret aims of Chief of Staff Röhm . . . (that is):

1 The present regime in Germany is not to be tolerated.
2 Above all, the Army and all national associations must be united in a single band.
3 The only man to be considered for such a position is Chief of Staff Röhm. . .

In the State there is only one bearer of arms-the Army; there is only one bearer of the political will-the National Socialist Party. . .

From Hitler's speech to the Reichstag, 13 July 1934

I Reactions to the Purge

The immediate result of the murders was great confusion, both as regards the way they were viewed and as regards their future political consequences. On the whole, Hitler's courage in taking decisive action was stressed the most. He was regarded practically as a hero. . . Our comrades report that Hitler has won strong approval and sympathy from that part of the population which still places its hopes in him. To these people his action is proof that he wants order and decency. Other sections of the population have been given cause for thought.

East Saxony: A small businessman told me that he and his colleagues had known for a long time that Hitler was going to strike at Röhm and his associates. He still sees Hitler, even now, as an utterly honourable man who wants the best for the German people. . . When I tried to explain to him that Hitler alone bore the responsibility for all the murders, these and earlier ones, he said: 'Still, the main thing is, he's got rid of the Marxists.'. . .

Bavaria: First report. By slaughtering his 'best friends', Hitler has forfeited none of his mass support as yet; rather he has gained. Reports from different parts of Bavaria are unanimous that people are expressing satisfaction that Hitler has acted so decisively. He has produced fresh proof that he will not settle for second-best and that he wants decency in public life.

From a report by the German Social Democratic Party in exile, following the Purge of 30 June 1934

J Hitler's Thanks
In consideration of the great services rendered by the SS, especially in connection with the events of 30 June 1934, I raise it to the status of an independent organisation within the framework of the NSDAP.

Decree concerning the SS, 20 July 1934

Questions

1 In what circumstances did Hitler issue the appeal outlined in Source A? **(2 marks)**

2 Using your own knowledge and the Source, explain the significance of Hitler's programme as outlined in Source A. **(6 marks)**

3 a Why was the Appeal in Source B issued at that particular time? **(2 marks)**

  b Comment on the content and tone of Source B. **(5 marks)**

4 Compare and contrast Sources A, B and C as types of Nazi propaganda. **(7 marks)**

5 Using your own knowledge and Sources D, E and F, estimate the importance of the measures outlined to the establishment of a Nazi dictatorship. **(8 marks)**

6 Using Source G and your own knowledge, explain why Hitler regarded the SA as a threat. **(6 marks)**

7 What are the uses and limitations of Sources H and I as evidence of the events surrounding the Purge of 30 June 1934? **(8 marks)**

8 Explain the reference to 'the great services rendered by the SS' in Source J. **(3 marks)**

9 Using *only* the evidence of Sources A–J, analyse the assertion that 'Hitler showed remarkable skill in establishing his dictatorship in the eighteen months following his accession to the Chancellorship.'
(12 marks)

3 THE NAZI PARTY

Hitler's accession to power in 1933 did not bring the Nazi Party quite the rewards that many of its more zealous members had expected. Certainly under the law of 14 July 1933 Germany was declared a one-party state, but the Nazi Party never attained quite the degree of authority that, for example, the Communist Party achieved in the Soviet Union. Germany in 1933 already contained a large and effective bureaucracy and, although Nazis took over many leading positions, old ideas and traditions died hard.

Another factor which inhibited the growth of a monolithic state was the existence of different interest groups and sections within the Party itself (for example the Hitler Youth), which often appealed to different sections of society. The Gauleiters, Hitler's regional governors, frequently complained of the difficulty of organising and directing the Party as a coherent whole within their areas of responsibility. Different structures abounded, often with little co-ordination: for example, by 1933 the SS was only nominally subordinate to the much larger SA. After 1933 many Party leaders were absorbed into government positions, which then occupied more of their attention than their Party posts. The Gauleiters themselves often operated independently of other authorities, recognising Hitler's power alone.

Hitler did express his own views on the role of the Party: it was essentially the guardian of ideology, with the task of preparing the German population psychologically for war and to accept Nazi racial doctrines. Hitler tended to remain aloof from internecine Party quarrels, whilst regarding the Party as his very 'own' instrument.

The Party carried out important but mundane tasks such as supervising the political morality of German citizens, for example by appointing block leaders to supervise groups of households.

Many rank and file Nazis detested the civil service and administration, believing them to be elitist and claiming that they typified the divisive class structure of pre-Nazi Germany and obstructed the implementation of radical social policies. Yet not all Party members were ideologically committed: much of the vast increase in Party membership from 1933 onwards was made up of opportunists, who swamped the 'old fighters', many of whom became disillusioned by the failure of the Party to deliver a radical revolution.

Members of the Nazi hierarchy itself often found their powers limited. Even Bormann failed to dominate completely either state or Party. (Hitler maintained personal channels of communication with individuals like Goebbels, and by-passed 'official' channels.)

The Nazi Party undoubtedly played an important role during the War, trying to sustain morale, and bearing the brunt of popular dissatisfaction in the later stages; but the dilemma of trying to mould a Party which was both an efficient administrative bureaucracy and a dynamic political movement was never really resolved.

A Hitler's Style of Leadership

In 1935 Hitler kept to a reasonably ordered daily routine. . . Gradually, this fairly orderly work routine broke down. . . He disliked the study of documents. I have sometimes secured decisions from him, even ones about important matters, without his ever asking to see the relevant files. He took the view that many things sorted themselves out on their own if one did not interfere. . . But the question was how did they sort themselves out? The Party leaders found it easiest to get something out of him. If they belonged to the top ranks they could always come to lunch. . . It was not surprising that the State offices were outmanoeuvred. . . He let people tell him the things he wanted to hear, everything else he rejected. One still sometimes hears the view that Hitler would have done the right thing if the people surrounding him had not kept him wrongly informed. Hitler refused to let himself be informed.

From the memoirs of Fritz Wiedemann, one of Hitler's Adjutants (1965)

B Another View of Hitler's Leadership

In the twelve years of his rule in Germany Hitler produced the biggest confusion in government that has ever existed in a civilised state. During his period of government, he removed from the organisation of the state all clarity of leadership and produced a completely opaque network of competences. It was not all laziness or an excessive degree of tolerance which led the otherwise so energetic and forceful Hitler to tolerate this real witch's cauldron of struggles for position and conflicts over competence. It was intentional. With this technique he systematically disorganised the upper echelons of the Reich leadership in order to develop and further the authority of his own will until it became a despotic tyranny.

From *Twelve Years With Hitler*, the memoirs of Otto Dietrich, Hitler's Press Chief (1955)

C The Tasks of the Party

The Führer stressed:
The most essential tasks of the Party were:

1 To make the people receptive for the measures intended by the Government;
2 To help carry out the measures which have been ordered by the Government in the nation at large;
3 To support the Government in every way. . .

The Führer described our main immediate task as the selection of people who were on the one hand able, and on the other hand willing, to carry out the Government's measures with blind obedience. The Party must bring about the stability on which Germany's whole future depended. . .

There must therefore be no superfluous discussions! Problems not yet decided by individual officials must under no circumstances be discussed in public. Otherwise, this will mean passing the decision on to the mass of the people. This was the crazy idea behind democracy. By doing that, the value of any leadership is squandered.

From Hitler's address to a conference of Gauleiters, 2 February 1934

D The Party and the State
(i) The leadership-state always has anti-liberal features; and it can also never be moulded and fashioned by the liberal type of man, but only by the type of men who are ever conscious of their inner union with folk and state. . . The German leadership-state must therefore imprint the National Socialist political ideology on the whole folk as its common attitude.

From Otto Koellreutter: *The German Leader-State* (1934)

(ii) . . . notions of liability . . . cannot be applied to the Party or the SA. Nor, equally, may the courts interfere under any pretext in the internal affairs and decisions of the Party organisation and thus infringe its leader-principle from outside. . . The Party, responsible only to itself, must develop its own standards from within.

Carl Schmitt, a Nazi legal expert (1933)

(iii) Although the identity of Party and State must be our ultimate aim, the realisation of this aim is at the moment a long way off. . . The influence of the Party on the State and the permeation of the State with National Socialist ideas does not correspond with the sacrifices made by the movement. The last few months in particular show a considerable decrease in the rate of growth of National Socialist influence upon the State.

From a memorandum by Hans Von Helms, a Nazi civil servant,
26 May 1934

(iv) Party offices have no authority whatever to issue instructions to agencies of the State. These agencies receive their instructions solely from their superiors within the State apparatus. . . People who interpreted the Führer's well-known statement 'It is not the State which commands but rather we who command the State' to mean that the Party was thereby made superior to the State, have completely misunderstood him. This statement merely implies that the leaders of the Party fill the top posts in the State and govern it. The Party organisation and the State apparatus are the two pillars of the State. The State is, therefore, the more all-embracing concept. The relationship between the two is defined even more clearly by the fact that the Party offices have no direct executive power because otherwise a disastrous duplication and parallel government would develop.

From a statement by the Reich Minister of the Interior, 1934

E Führer Power
The position of the Führer combines in itself all sovereign power of the Reich; all public power in the State, as in the movement, is derived from the Führer power. If we wish to define political power in the *volkish* Reich correctly, we must not speak of 'State power' but of 'Führer power'.

From E. Huber: *Constitutional Law in the Great German Reich*, 1939

Questions

1 To what extent does Source B support Source A in its impression of the system of government employed by Hitler in the Third Reich?

(6 marks)

2 How would an historian assess the reliability of either Source A or Source B as evidence of the method of government in the Third Reich?

(4 marks)

3 What was Hitler's conception of the role of the Party in the Nazi State, as outlined in Source C? **(5 marks)**

4 To what extent do the extracts in Source D support each other in their view of the role of the Party in the Nazi state? **(8 marks)**

5 Using Sources A–E, and your own knowledge, assess the validity of Neumann's claim that the Third Reich was 'a nonstate, a chaos, a situation of lawlessness, disorder and anarchy.' **(12 marks)**

4 THE ECONOMY

It is difficult to be precise about the aims of Nazi economic policy since the policy itself had never been coherent. It was really a collection of prejudices (as expressed in the Twenty-Five Point Programme) and (sometimes mutually antagonistic) ideas such as the creation of a self-sufficient economy, which implied rigorous controls, alongside a reluctance to alienate working-class supporters which might follow the introduction of rationing and other politically unpopular measures.

Not all of Hitler's economic policies were original. He continued, admittedly on a grander scale, the policy of previous governments of spending money on public works and subsidies in order to reduce unemployment. Rearmament, public works, the discouragement of female labour, and a general improvement in world trade, all helped to abolish unemployment by 1939.

Other hopes were less easy to fulfil. Attempts to give security to peasants and farmers, for example, made it difficult to promote large-scale modern farming methods. Promises to prevent the encroachment of big department stores on small traders and to prevent the development of cartels and other manifestations of big business clashed with Hitler's desire for business support and the rearmament drive.

Schacht, Hitler's President of the Reichsbank, introduced various schemes to finance rearmament and achieve self-sufficiency. Such schemes involved favourable trade deals with other countries and the regulation of imports and currency. Hermann Göring introduced a Four Year Plan, which was designed to prepare Germany for war by making her self-sufficient. Some successes were achieved in the development of synthetic materials which would obviate the need for imports, but production targets were not met and bureaucratic muddling and lack of coordinated direction undermined some of the original hopes.

Although the State increased its powers over the economy, large-scale capitalism did not suffer. Some large firms even managed to strengthen their monopoly position. Industry as a whole expanded, profits increased considerably, and many firms profited from the initial German successes in taking over foreign enterprises after the victorious military campaigns of 1940-1.

A The Nazi Economic Programme
We demand land and territory for the nourishment of our people and for settling our surplus population. . .

We demand the abolition of incomes unearned by work.

We demand that there shall be profit-sharing in the great industries. . .

We demand . . . the passing of a law for the confiscation without compensation of land for communal purposes . . . and prohibition of all speculation in land.

From the *Twenty-Five Point Programme of the Nazi Party*, 1920

B A Nazi View of Economic Priorities
This great anti-capitalist longing – as I call it – which is going through our nation and which has gripped perhaps as many as 95 per cent of our people is interesting and valuable . . . (it is) proof of the fact that we are on the threshold of a great, a tremendous new epoch: the overcoming of liberalism and the emergence of a new kind of economic thinking and a new attitude to the State. . .

Germany is still dependent on foreign countries for the most important human need: namely foodstuffs. A nation which is dependent on foreign countries is in the final analysis never in a position to solve its foreign policy problems, the problems of its economic freedom as it would wish. In other words, we must enable sufficient essential foodstuffs to be produced on German soil to feed the whole population. One should have done that before the present level of unemployment was reached, as a response to the Treaty of Versailles which reduced our living space and which should have automatically produced a response in the form of a reorganisation of agricultural production. In addition, we need in Germany an ambitious housing and population policy, ie the resettlement of people away from the big cities.

From a speech by Gregor Strasser in the Reichstag, 10 May 1932

C Hitler's Economic Plans
Germany's economic situation is . . . in the briefest outline as follows: we are overpopulated and cannot feed ourselves from our own resources . . . the most important task of our economic policy is to see that all Germans are incorporated into the economic process . . . the yield of our agricultural production can undergo no further substantial increase. It is equally impossible for us, at present, to manufacture artificially certain raw materials which we lack in Germany or to find other substitutes for them. . . The final solution lies in extending our living space, that is to say, extending the sources of raw materials and foodstuffs of our people. . . There is only one interest,

the interest of the nation; only one view, the bringing of Germany to the point of political and economic self-sufficiency. . .

I thus set the following tasks:

1 The German armed forces must be operational within four years.
2 The German economy must be fit for war within four years.

From a memorandum composed by Hitler, August 1936

D Economic Planning and Reality

Commodity	Output (thousand tons)			Plan target
	1936	*1938*	*1942*	
Oil	1,790	2,340	6,260	13,830
Aluminium	98	166	260	273
Buna rubber	0.7	5	96	120
Nitrogen	770	914	930	1,040
Explosives	18	45	300	323
Powder	20	26	150	217
Steel	19,216	22,656	20,480	24,000
Iron ore	2,255	3,360	4,137	5,549
Brown coal	161,382	194,985	245,918	240,500
Hard coal	158,400	186,186	166,059	213,000

Figures from the Four Year Plan, launched in 1936

E Complaints about Nazi Economic Policy

The small businessmen are in a state of gloom and despondency. These people, to whom the present system to a large extent owes its rise, are the most disappointed of all. The shortages of goods restrict their turnover, but they cannot respond by putting up their prices because the price decrees prevent them from doing so. The artisans complain about raw material shortages . . . one can say of many of them (the small businessmen) that inwardly they have long since turned away from the system and would welcome its fall.

From a report by the Social Democratic Party on the situation in central Germany, July 1939

F The Attitude of Farmers

The Entailed Farm Law has advantages as well as disadvantages just like the controlled market. Many peasants find it difficult to distinguish between advantages and disadvantages. They grumble non-stop and many are under heavier financial pressure than before, but others are better off. The peasants are more upset by the regime's fight against Christianity than by economic difficulties. . . They wanted nothing to do with Communism – at least the peasants with medium-sized farms didn't. They were afraid that Bolshevism would take away their land and they would prefer to come to terms with the Nazis who only dispossess them of half their property.

From a report by the Social Democratic Party on the situation in Bavaria, August 1937

G Statistics on Earnings
Average gross hourly earnings in industry

(a) In Reichspfennig

Industry	Gross hourly earnings (Reichspfennig)			
	1935	*1936*	*1937*	*1938*
Building	72.4	72.1	72.3	75.4
Chemicals	82.0	82.0	84.6	85.3
Iron and Steel	–	86.3	93.5	96.1
Rubber	–	–	–	87.8
Metal-working	83.6	85.7	88.9	91.1
Quarrying	–	–	60.1	73.7
Clothing	53.8	54.5	55.7	59.6
Textiles	55.0	54.6	55.8	59.1
Boots and Shoes	62.3	63.2	64.7	66.5
All industries	73.6	76.7	78.2	81.0

(b) Indexed at 1936 = 100

1928 = 122.9	1934 = 97
1929 = 129.5	1935 = 99.4
1930 = 125.8	1936 = 100
1931 = 116.3	1937 = 102.0
1932 = 97.6	1938 = 105.6
1933 = 94.6	

From official German sources

Questions

1 To what extent do Sources B and C reflect the economic concerns expressed in Source A? **(6 marks)**

2 Using Source D, estimate the success of the Four Year Plan. **(4 marks)**

3 What are the uses and limitations of Sources E and F for an understanding of the impact of Nazi economic policy?   **(6 marks)**

4 How would an historian assess the reliability of the information in Source G?   **(4 marks)**

5 Using the Sources *and* your own knowledge, assess the validity of the claim that 'By 1939, an economic crisis was just around the corner for Germany.'   **(10 marks)**

5 PROPAGANDA

Propaganda was always an integral weapon in the Nazi armoury of methods to gain and keep support. Hitler himself had been a propaganda expert in the early days of the Party, and some of the most interesting passages in *Mein Kampf* concern the nature and purpose of propaganda. Josef Goebbels founded the Nazi Party Reich Propaganda Directorate in 1930, and headed the new Ministry of Public Enlightenment and Propaganda formed in March 1933. Goebbels, a propagandist of genius, saw propaganda as fulfilling a dynamic role in mobilising support for the Nazis among the entire population, and he also wished to control culture in its broadest sense.

A variety of propaganda techniques was employed by the Nazis to get their message across to a literate, well-educated population. The radio was regarded as an especially effective medium, although Goebbels had to overcome resistance from within and without the Party before he could establish effective control. Listening to the radio was actively encouraged, and entertainment as well as direct political propaganda was transmitted.

It proved less easy to first muzzle and then take over the German press, because German newspapers were controlled by a variety of parties, interest groups, individuals and companies. Laws were passed to strengthen the role of editors which, at the same time, increased their subordination to the State. The Reich Press Chamber enforced State controls. The Nazis increased their holdings of newspapers, and by the late 1930s all aspects of newspaper ownership and publication were strictly controlled by the Nazis.

Propaganda was often an intregral component of films, the school curriculum, Nazi organisations like the Hitler Youth, rituals, and movements like 'Winter Relief'. However, research in recent years suggests that the effectiveness of propaganda in terms of directly influencing the attitudes of the German people towards issues such as anti-semitism may have been overestimated.

A Goebbels on the Role of the Ministry of Public Enlightenment and Propaganda

I view the first tasks of the new Ministry as being to establish co-ordination between the Government and the whole people. If this government is determined never and under no circumstances to give way, then it has no need of the lifeless power of the bayonet, and in the long run will not be content with 52 per cent behind it and with terrorising the remaining 48 per cent, but will see its most immediate tasks as being to win over that remaining 48 per cent...

It is not enough for people to be more or less reconciled to our regime, to be persuaded to adopt a neutral attitude towards us. Rather we want to work on people until they have capitulated to us, until they grasp ideologically that what is happening in Germany today not only *must* be accepted but also *can* be accepted.

Propaganda is not an end in iself, but a means to an end. If the means achieves the end then the means is good... The new Ministry has no other aim than to unite the nation behind the ideal of the national revolution...

The most important tasks of this Ministry must be the following: first, all propaganda ventures and all institutions of public information belonging to the Reich and the states must be centralised in one hand. Furthermore, it must be our task to instil into these propaganda facilities a modern feeling and bring them up to date ... the leaders of today must be modern princes of the people, they must be able to understand the people but need not follow them slavishly. It is their duty to tell the masses what they want and put it across to the masses in such a way that they understand it too.

From a speech by Goebbels at his first press conference, 15 March 1933

B The Radio as Propaganda
I consider radio to be the most modern and the most crucial instrument that exists for influencing the masses. I also believe – one should not say that out loud – that radio will, in the end, replace the press...

First principle: At all costs avoid being boring. I put that before everything... You must help to bring forth a nationalist art and culture which is truly appropriate to the pace of modern life and to the mood of the times... You must use your imagination, an imagination which is based on sure foundations and which employs all means and methods to bring to the ears of the masses the new attitude in a way which is modern, up-to-date, interesting, and appealing; interesting, instructive but not schoolmasterish.

From instructions by Goebbels to the controllers of German radio, 25 March 1933

C The Press as Propaganda
... The press is not only there to inform but must also instruct... I am aware of the significance of the press. I recognise what it means for a government to have a good press or a bad press... You need not be afraid of making statements with obvious bias. There is

nothing unbiased in the world. Anything unbiased is sexless and thus worthless. Everything has a bias whether acknowledged or concealed. In my view it is better for us to acknowledge our bias rather than conceal it. There is no absolute objectivity.

From Goebbels' announcement at his first press conference,
15 March 1933

D Propaganda for the Followers

We have witnessed many great march-pasts and ceremonies. But none of them was more thrilling, and at the same time more inspiring, than yesterday's roll call of the 140,000 political wardens, who were addressed by the Führer at night, on the Zeppelin Meadow which floodlights had made bright as day. It is hardly possible to let words describe the mood and strength of this hour. . .

A distant roar becomes stronger and comes even closer. The Führer is there! Reich Organizational Leader, Dr Ley, gives him the report on the men who are standing in parade formation. And then, a great surprise, one among many. As Adolf Hitler is entering the Zeppelin Field, 150 floodlights of the air force blaze up. They are distributed around the entire square, and cut into the night, erecting a canopy of light in the midst of darkness. . . The wide field resembles a powerful Gothic cathedral made of light. Bluish-violet shine the floodlights, and between their cone of light hangs the dark cloth of night. . . Twenty-five thousand flags, that means 25,000 local, district, and factory groups all over the nation who are gathered around this flag. Every one of these flag bearers is ready to give his life in the defence of every one of these pieces of cloth. There is no one among them to whom this flag is not the final command and the highest obligation. . . A devotional hour of the Movement is being held here, is protected by a sea of light against the darkness outside.

The men's arms are lifted in salute, which at this moment goes out to the dead of the Movement and of the War. Then the flags are raised again.

Dr Ley speaks: 'We believe in a Lord God, who directs us and guides us, and who has sent to us you, my Führer.' These are the final words of the Reich Organizational leader; they are underlined by the applause that rises from the 150,000 spectators and that lasts for minutes.

From a description of the roll-call of Political Wardens (Heads of local Party groups) at the 1936 Nuremberg Rally, reported in *Niederelbisches Tageblatt*, 12 September 1936

E A torchlit parade in Berlin, 1938, celebrating the fifth
anniversary of the Nazi accession to power

F Photograph of Hitler, Goebbels and children

G 'National Socialism. The organised will of the nation.' 1932
election poster

H 'We farmers are mucking out. We vote List 2 National Socialist.'
Poster produced for the 1932 elections

| 'Loyalty, Honour and Order'. 1934 Nazi poster

J 'The entire people says "Yes" (on 10 April).' Produced for the Plebiscite following the Austro-German *Anschluss* of 1938

K Poster advertising the Pomerania District Rally of the NSDAP,
Stettin, 10–12 June 1938

L 'Building youth hostels and homes.' Poster designed in 1938 or
1939 for a street collection for youth hostels, organised by the
Association of German Youth Hostels (a subsidiary organisation
of the Hitler Youth)

M 'Service in the SA develops comradeship, toughness, strength!'
Produced in 1941 as part of a wall-newspaper to be displayed
in offices and schools

N 'Adolf Hitler is victory'. Poster designed in 1943 for display in offices and schoolrooms

O Poster designed to advertise the film 'The Wandering Jew'
during the Second World War

P 'What awaits us next?' Nazi poster from 1944 listing defeats inflicted on the French by the English between 1300 and 1942

Questions

1 What information can be gleaned from Sources A, B and C about Goebbels' views on the aims and methods of Nazi propaganda?

(8 marks)

2 Identify the elements of propaganda that can be found in Sources D, E and F. **(6 marks)**

3 Study Sources G–P. For each of these Sources:
(i) Identify the main theme of the Source; **(10 marks)**
(ii) Explain how the propaganda message is put across. **(10 marks)**

4 Select any three examples from Sources A–P and, for each example, explain its uses and limitations to an historian of Nazi Germany.

(12 marks)

6 EDUCATION AND YOUTH

Germany had long held a reputation in Europe for high educational standards. The Nazis did not therefore face the problem which confronted the Communists in Russia, that of educating a largely illiterate population in order to be receptive to the regime's propaganda and to provide a modern, efficient work-force. In fact, the Nazis made few drastic changes in the structure of the German educational system, although they did revise syllabuses so that subjects were given a Nazi ideological slant. Also, some subjects like sport and biology received a special impetus, Girls recived fewer opportunities to attend grammar schools, and some special schools were created to train the future elite.

Educational standards almost certainly dropped during Nazi rule. Not only was this due to the increasingly propagandist element in education, but also to the fact that a climate of anti-intellectualism was deliberately fostered, extra-curricular activities increasingly impinged upon the curriculum, and organisations such as the Hitler Youth exercised more appeal for some people than the classroom. Teachers experienced a decline in prestige and recruitment to the profession fell. Contemporary reports testified to the drop in educational standards.

The Nazi movement had always incorporated a substantial youth following, attracted by the dynamic image, and the Nazi State inevitably devoted considerable attention to the activities of the young. Youth was regimented in a network of organisations for boys and girls. These organisations, notably the Hitler Youth, inculcated propaganda, sport, and a sense of 'belonging', whilst the girls' organisations devoted more time to 'traditional' domestic skills.

Ironically, in view of the Nazi concern for youth, life for many young people proved difficult in the 1930s. Large numbers of children worked in industry from the age of fourteen and the health of young people appears to have declined. Reserves of youthful idealism were certainly tapped by the youth organisations, but many young people appear to have resented the regimentation which membership of these organisations entailed.

A 'Unity of Youth in the Hitler Youth'. A propaganda poster for
the Hitler Youth

B Hitler's Ideas on Youth

There were times, which now seem to us very far off and almost incomprehensible, when the ideal of the young man was the chap who could hold his beer and was good for a drink. But now his day is past and we like to see not the man who can hold his drink, but the young man who can stand all weathers – the hardened young man. Because what matters is not how many glasses of beer he can drink, but how many blows he can stand; not how many nights he can spend on the spree, but how many kilometres he can march. . .

What we look for from our German youth is different from what people wanted in the past. In our eyes the German youth of the future must be slim and slender, swift as the greyhound, tough as leather, and hard as Krupp steel.

From Hitler's speech at the Nuremburg Party Rally, 14 September 1935

C Membership of the Youth Movement

	Hitler Youth (14–18)	German Young People (10–14)	League of German Girls (14–18)	League of Young Girls (10–14)	Total	Total population of 10–18 year olds
1932	55,365	28,691	19,244	4,656	107,956	
1933	568,288	1,130,521	243,750	349,482	2,292,041	7,529,000
1934	786,000	1,457,304	471,944	862,317	3,577,565	7,682,000
1935	829,361	1,498,209	569,599	1,046,134	3,943,303	8,172,000
1936	1,168,734	1,785,424	873,127	1,610,316	5,437,601	8,656,000
1937	1,237,078	1,884,883	1,035,804	1,722,190	5,879,955	9,060,000
1938	1,663,305	2,064,538	1,448,264	1,855,119	7,031,226	9,109,000
1939	1,723,886	2,137,594	1,502,571	1,923,419	7,287,470	8,870,000

Adapted from official German sources

D Reasons for Joining the Hitler Youth

There were boys from all classes of families, though mainly middle class and workers. There were no social or class distinctions, which I approved of very much. There was no direct or obvious political indoctrination until later – after Hitler came to power. . . We did march in parades and hated the SPD, but that was all general, not specific – it was all a part of it.

From a recollection of a Hitler Youth member, quoted in W. Allen, *The Nazi Seizure Of Power* (1984)

E Recollections of a BDM Leader

The Hitler Youth was a youth organisation. Its members may have allowed themselves to be dressed in uniforms and regimented, but they were still young people and they behaved like young people.

Their characteristic surplus of energy and thirst for action found great scope in their programme of activities, which constantly required great feats to be performed. It was part of the method of the National Socialist Youth leadership to arrange almost everything in the form of competitions. . . Every unit wanted to have the best group 'home', the most interesting expedition log, the biggest collection for the Winter Relief Fund, and so forth. . . There was certainly a great deal of good and ambitious education in the Hitler Youth. There were groups who learned to act in a masterly way. People told stories, danced and practised handicrafts, and in these fields the regimentation was fortunately often less strict.

From M. Maschmann: *Account Rendered* (1964)

F The Appeal of the Hitler Youth

Youth is still in favour of the system: the novelty, the drill, the uniform, the camp life, the fact that school and the parental home take a back seat compared to the community of young people – all that is marvellous. . . Many believe that they will find job opportunities through the persecution of Jews and Marxists. . . For the first time, peasant youth is associated with the State through the SA and the Hitler Youth. Young workers also join in: one day Socialism may come; one is simply trying to achieve it in a new way. . . The new generation has never had much use for education and reading. Now nothing is demanded of them; on the contrary, knowledge is publicly condemned. . .

It is the young men who bring home enthusiasm for the Nazis. Old men make no impression nowadays. . . I am almost inclined to say that the secret of National Socialism is the secret of its youth. The chaps are so fanaticised that they believe in nothing but their Hitler.

From reports by the Social Democratic Party in exile, 1934

G Further Recollections of the Youth Movement

(i) When I became a leader in the *Jungvolk* the negative aspects became very obvious. I found the compulsion and the requirement of absolute obedience unpleasant. I appreciated that there must be order and discipline in such a large group of boys, but it was exaggerated. It was preferred that people should not have a will of their own and should totally subordinate themselves . . . when I moved to Bann headquarters and acquired rather more insight I had the first serious doubts. The Hitler Youth was interfering everywhere in people's private lives. If one had private interests apart from the Hitler Youth people looked askance.

From A. Klonne: *Youth in the Third Reich* (1982)

(ii) Young people are more easily influenced in terms of mood than are adults. This fact made it easier for the regime to win over young people in the first years after the seizure of power. It appears that the same fact is now making it hard for the regime to keep young people in thrall. . . They were made particularly large promises which for the most part were incapable of fulfilment. The great mass of young people today can see that the well-paying posts in public administration and the Party apparatus have been filled by comrades who had the good fortune of being a few years older. . . In the long run young people too are feeling increasingly irritated by the lack of freedom and the mindless drilling that is customary in the National Socialist organisations. . .

Both boys and girls are trying by every means possible to dodge the year of Land Service. . . There is a section of youth that wants the romantic life. Whole bundles of trashy literature have been found in small caves. Apprentices too are disappearing from home much more frequently. . .

From a report from the Social Democratic Party in exile, 1938

H The Teaching of History
The German nation in its essence and greatness, in its fateful struggle for internal and external identity is the subject of the teaching of history. It is based on the natural bond of the child with his nation and, by interpreting history as the fateful struggle for existence between the nations, has the particular task of educating young people to respect the great German past and to have faith in the mission and future of their own nation and to respect the right of existence of other nations.

From official instructions on the teaching of history, issued by the German Central Institute of Education, 1938

I Some Maths Problems
The construction of a lunatic asylum costs 6 million RM. How many houses at 15,000 RM each could have been built for that amount?

A modern night bomber can carry 1,800 incendiaries. How long (in kilometres) is the path along which it can distribute these bombs if it drops a bomb every second at a speed of 250 km per hour? How far apart are the craters from one another? . . . How many fires are caused if $\frac{1}{3}$ of the bombs hit their targets and of these $\frac{1}{3}$ ignite?

Questions from mathematics textbooks published in the 1930s

J The Timetable in a Girls' School

	Monday	Tuesday	Wednesday	Thursday	Friday	Saturday
8.00–8.45	German	German	German	German	German	German
8.50–9.35	Geography	History	Singing	Geography	History	Singing
9.40–10.25	Race Study	Race Study	Race Study	Ideology	Ideology	Ideology
10.25–11.00	Break, with Sports and Special Announcements					
11.00–12.05	Domestic Science with Mathematics, daily					
12.10–12.55	Eugenics, alternating with Health Biology					

K A 'Nazi Novel'

At least a thousand youths were standing around a burning pile of wood; or perhaps it was only a hundred. But it was as though this circle of young people stretched to the very edges of the world. Just in front of him, marshalled in lines, stood youths like himself. Each held a long pole with a pennant, rising vertically to the sky, black pennants and brilliant red. . . Each of the youths looked like all the others, with shorts, bare knees, brown shirt, a kerchief around the neck. . .

They were all looking in silence towards the fire. A tall young man had taken his stand beside it and was speaking to them. . . Heini could make out only a few phrases: he heard the words 'movement' and 'leader', he heard part of a sentence – 'each giving his life for the others'. As he listened, wondering whether he might not creep a little closer to hear better, a great thrill of fear went through him. *'Deutschland, Deutschland Über Alles'* swept over him, from a thousand voices, like a scalding wave. I too am a German, he thought; and he was filled with profound knowledge, stronger and more unexpected than anything he had felt in his life before. . . This was German soil, German forest, these were German youths; and he saw that he stood apart, alone, with no one to help him; and he did not know what to make of this great and sudden feeling.

From 'Hitlerjunge Quex'

Questions

1 What information about the Nazi ideal of youth can be gleaned from Sources A, B, D, E, and F? **(10 marks)**

2 What are the uses and limitations of Sources A, D and E to a social historian of the Third Reich? **(8 marks)**

3 What questions would an historian ask in order to assess the reliability of Source C? **(6 marks)**

4 Compare and contrast Sources D, E, F and G as evidence of the appeal of the Nazi youth movements to the youth of Germany.
(10 marks)

5 To what extent to Sources H, I and J prove that the Nazi education system was ideological in conception? **(8 marks)**

6 Using your own knowledge, assess the extent to which Source K is typical of Nazi propaganda aimed at youth during the 1930s.
(6 marks)

7 Using the Sources A–K and your own knowledge, assess the validity of the claim that 'Indoctrination of youth was one of the most important and successful planks of Nazi social policy during the Third Reich'. **(12 marks)**

7 ANTI-SEMITISM

Jews had been quite well assimilated into German life before the First World War, although there had been a wave of anti-semitism towards the end of the nineteenth century, fuelled by economic jealousy and a dislike of 'alien' intellectual influences with which Jews were popularly associated. The Weimar Republic was tolerant, but was branded as 'Jewish' by opponents such as the Nazis. The fact that a small proportion of Jews was prominent in political, economic and cultural life, provided opportunities for anti-semitic propaganda.

Debates have arisen over the extent to which the Nazis believed in their racial theories. To what extent were the latter a convenient means of providing a scapegoat and of winning the support of social groups like the lower middle classes, who felt threatened? Anti-semitic measures were not uncontrolled: although a boycott of Jewish civil servants and intellectuals was implemented within months of Hitler's accession to power, measures against doctors and even some Jewish businessmen were delayed because they performed a valuable role in the economy. Nevertheless, a process of public discrimination against the Jews and the deprival of rights under the Nuremberg Laws helped to prepare the Aryan population for the idea of the complete removal of Jewish influence from German life.

Reactions to the Pogrom of 1938 were mixed, yet few Germans would stand up for the Jews, even if most Germans were not as anti-semitic as the Nazi leadership.

Despite Hitler's repeated threats against 'World Jewry', the Nazi decision to eliminate Jews under their control was arrived at slowly. Once at war, it became Nazi dogma that the Jews were the real motive force behind Germany's enemies. Although the existence of extermination camps was kept secret as long as possible, the killing of Jews in occupied Europe had already begun in 1941, and detailed plans for the elimination of Europe's Jews were approved at the Wannsee Conference of 1942.

Ironically, a racial policy which, despite Nazi rantings, was implemented initially in a relatively controlled fashion, by the middle of the War had become such an obsession that operations by the SS against the Jews were even sometimes allowed to take precedence over operations important to military success.

An Anti-Semitic cartoon. From a German children's book, 1938

B Anti-Semitic Propaganda in School

Little Karl takes the pointer, goes to the blackboard and points to the sketches. 'A Jew is usually recognised by his nose. The Jewish nose is crooked at the end. . . Many non-Jews have crooked noses too. But their noses are bent, not at the end, but further up. Such a nose is called a hook nose or eagle's beak. It has nothing to do with a Jewish nose. . .

'The Jew is also recognised by his lips. His lips are usually thick. Often the lower lip hangs down. . . And the Jew is also recognised by his eyes. His eyelids are usually thicker and more fleshy than ours. The look of the Jew is sly and sharp'. . .

Inge sits in the Jew doctor's reception room. She has to wait a long time. She looks through the magazines on the table. But she is much too nervous even to read a few sentences. Again and again she remembers her talk with her mother. And again and again her mind dwells on the warnings of the BDM leader: 'A German must not consult a Jew doctor! And particularly not a German girl! Many a girl who has gone to a Jew doctor to be cured has found disease and disgrace!'. . .

The door opens. Inge looks up. There stands the Jew. She screams. She's so frightened, she drops the magazine. She jumps up in terror. Her eyes stare into the Jewish doctor's face. His face is the face of a devil. In the middle of this devil's face is a huge crooked nose. Behind the spectacles two criminal eyes. And the thick lips are grinning. A grin that says: 'Now I've got you at last, little German girl!'

Excerpts from a Nazi schoolbook: *The Poisonous Mushroom*, 1938

C The Impact of Anti-Semitic Propaganda

The Jewish laws are not taken very seriously because the population has other problems on its mind and is mostly of the opinion that the whole fuss about the Jews is only being made to divert people's attention from other things and to provide the SA with something to do. But one must not imagine that the anti-Jewish agitation does not have the desired effect on many people. On the contrary, there are enough people who are influenced by the defamation of the Jews and regard the Jews as the originators of many bad things. They have become fanatical opponents of the Jews. This emnity often finds expression in the form of spying on people and denouncing them for having dealing with Jews, probably in the hope of winning recognition and advantages from the Party. But the vast majority of the population ignore this defamation of the Jews; they even demonstratively prefer to buy in Jewish department stores and adopt a really unfriendly attitude to the SA men on duty there, particularly if they try and take photographs of people going in.

From a report by a Social Democrat supporter in Saxony, September 1935

D Popular Reaction to Anti-Semitic Excesses

The broad mass of the people has not condoned the destruction, but we should nevertheless not overlook the fact that there are people among the working class who do not defend the Jews. There are certain circles where you are not very popular if you speak disparagingly about the recent incidents. . . Berlin: the population's attitude was not fully unanimous. . . If there has been any speaking out in the Reich against the Jewish pogroms, the excesses of arson and looting, it has been in Hamburg and the neighbouring Elbe district. People from Hamburg are not generally anti-semitic, and the Hamburg Jews have been assimilated far more than the Jews in other parts of the Reich.

From a report by the German Social Democratic Party in Exile, December 1938

E A Hitler Prophecy

If the international Jewish financiers in and outside Europe should succeed in plunging the nations once more into a world war, then the result will not be the Bolshevising of the earth, and thus the victory of Jewry, but the annihilation of the Jewish race in Europe!

From a speech by Hitler to the Reichstag, 30 January 1939

F Goebbels Blames the Jews

The Jews wanted their war. Now they have it. But what is also coming true for them is the Führer's prophecy which he voiced in his Reichstag speech of 30 January 1939. . .

In this historic conflict every Jew is our enemy, no matter whether he is vegetating in a Polish ghetto, or still supporting his parasitical existence in Berlin or Hamburg, or blowing the war trumpet in New York or Washington. By reason of their birth and race, all Jews are members of an international conspiracy against National Socialist Germany. . . There is a difference between humans and humans, just as there is a difference between animals and animals. We know good and bad humans, just as we know good and bad animals. The fact that the Jew still lives among us is no proof that he is one of us, no more than the flea's domestic resilience makes him a domestic animal. . .

So superfluous though it might be, let me say once more:

The Jews are our destruction. They provoked and brought about this war. . . Every German soldier's death in this war is the Jews' responsibility. . . The Jews enjoy the protection of the enemy nations. No further proof is needed of their destructive role among our people.

From J. Goebbels' article 'The Jews Are to Blame' in *Das Reich*, 16 November, 1941

G The Final Solution

'The Jewish people will be exterminated', says every party comrade,
'It's clear, it's in our programme. Elimination of the Jews,
extermination and we'll do it.' And then they come along, the worthy
eighty million Germans, and each one of them produces his decent
Jew. It's clear the others are swine, but this one is a fine Jew. Not
one of those who talk like that has watched it happening, not one of
them has been through it. Most of you will know what it means when
a hundred corpses are lying side by side, or five hundred or a
thousand are lying there. To have stuck it out and – apart from a few
exceptions due to human weakness – to have remained decent, that is
what has made us tough. . . We had the moral right, we had the duty
to our people, to destroy this people which wanted to destroy us.
But we have not the right to enrich ourselves with so much as a fur,
a watch, a mark, a cigarette or anything else. We have exterminated
a bacterium because we do not want in the end to be infected by the
bacterium and die of it. . . All in all, we can say that we have fulfilled
this most difficult duty for the love of our people. And our spirit, our
soul. Our character has not suffered injury from it.

From a speech by Himmler to SS Leaders at Posen, 4 October 1943

Questions

1 Using Sources A and B, and your own knowledge, explain the
methods by which the Nazis promoted anti-semitic propaganda in
Germany during the 1930s. **(8 marks)**

2 Using your own knowledge, explain the reference to 'Jewish laws' in
Source C. **(3 marks)**

3 Using your own knowledge, explain the references to the 'recent
incidents' and 'Jewish pogroms' in Source D. **(4 marks)**

4 To what extent do Sources C and D suggest that anti-semitic
propaganda was effective in influencing the German population?
(6 marks)

5 What questions might an historian ask in order to evaluate the
reliability of Sources C and D? **(4 marks)**

6 What evidence of propaganda is contained in Sources E and F?
(6 marks)

7 Using your own knowledge, explain the role of Himmler and the SS
in the Final Solution. **(7 marks)**

8 Using only the evidence of Sources A–G, assess the validity of the statement that 'anti-semitism was less of a genuine belief of the Nazis than a convenient weapon to support or excuse their policies.'

(8 marks)

8 CULTURE

As in Soviet Russia, culture was regarded not just as an expression of aesthetic feeling but as a moralising, didactic force which existed to serve the needs of the regime. Although Alfred Rosenberg had long been the acknowledged Party 'expert' on ideology and culture, after 1933 Goebbels fought to establish control of culture himself. Goebbels succeeded chiefly because he controlled the Reich Chamber of Culture, established in September 1933. This position enabled him to promote his views at a State as well as at a Party level. All professional actors, musicians, artists and writers were obliged to belong to the Chamber in order to practise their craft, and Goebbels could control their admission on grounds of suitability.

Hitler also had his own dogmatic opinions on art and set the tone for Nazi cultural policy, although some notable events like the burning of the books (May 1933) were semi-official in origin rather than being directly organised by the regime itself. Hitler did proclaim art to be an expression of the true German spirit and opposed modernism and other 'unGermanic' tendencies.

Inevitably, cultural life in the Third Reich suffered. This was not just due to censorship itself, but also to the fact that many great intellectuals emigrated or kept silent. Nazi attempts to encourage their own or 'people's culture' met with little success in an already culturally-sophisticated nation, although the output of books in particular was prodigious during the life of the Third Reich.

A 'The Burning of the Books'
Against class struggle and materialism.
For the national community and an idealistic outlook.
Marx, Kautsky.

Against decadence and moral decay.
For discipline and morality in family and state.
H. Mann, Ernst Glaeser, E. Kastner.

Against the falsification of our history and the denigration of its great figures.
For awe for our past.
Emil Ludwig, Werner Hegemann.

Against alien journalism of a democratic-Jewish stamp.
For responsible participation in the work of national reconstruction.
Theodor Wolff, Georg Bernhard.

Against literary betrayal of the soldiers of the World War.
For the education of the nation in the spirit of military preparedness.
E. Remarque.

'Fire Spells' recited during the 'Ritual Burning of the Books' in Berlin,
10 May 1933

B Unsuitable Literature
Ilse-Lore Danner, *Susan Makes Her Way*
Describes the seduction of minors, a danger to German youth.

Fritz Sander, *Fight For The City*
The heroes are hoodlums and murderers.

Some of the books listed by the Ministry of Propaganda during one week
in July 1940

C German Physics?
In reality science, like everything created by men, is race-conditioned,
blood-conditioned. An illusion of internationality can arise if people
wrongly conclude from the general validity of the results of natural
science that its origins are also general; or if they overlook the fact
that the peoples of various countries who have handed down
knowledge of the same sort as the German people, or of a similar
sort, have been able to do this only because and in so far as they are,
or were, at the same time of a predominantly nordic racial mixture.
Peoples of a different racial mixture have a different way of pursuing
knowledge.

From 'German Physics', an essay by the Nobel Prizewinner, Professor
Philipp Lenard, 1936

D Nazi Humour
It is easier to show by practical example than by theoretical discussion
where the ever necessary consideration of the interests of state and
nation has been forgotten. If – without, for the time being, mentioning
names – we give such examples of clumsy editorial work, we do so in
order to prevent similar accidents in future.

A Sad Joke
An illustrated magazine recently ran the following 'joke' on its
humour page:
   The passengers of an ocean liner are whiling away the time with
shipboard games. One gentleman steps up to another and says, 'We
are having a race now between married and unmarrieds. You are
married, aren't you?' 'No,' says the other, 'I only look that way, I am
seasick.'

Quid Pro Quo

A humour magazine had a similar story to offer:
    First guest of the hunt: 'The devil! You nearly hit my wife, Sir!'
    Second guest: 'So sorry! Look, why don't you have a shot at mine!'

Even if one is very broad minded, and has a great basic sense of humour, one must be astonished at how these magazines — at a time of our vital and bitterly serious struggle to strengthen the family, and to bring our entire life into line with the policy on population and race — can commit such a blunder.

The Jewish joke must disappear, and be replaced by a truly German, positive humour. A good example of how it can be done was a caricature we recently saw which showed the sufferings of the only bachelor in his block.

From confidential instructions issued by the Ministry of Propaganda to Periodical Editors, May 1939

E The Ideal Aryan Family: Poster issued by the Office of Racial Politics of the NSDAP, 1938

F Ideal Aryan Types: Adolf Ziegler's painting 'The Judgement of Paris'

G The Ideal German Girl: Paul Keck's painting, exhibited in 1939

H The German Hero: Arno Brecker's 'The Guardian'

I Active Youth: Mural by Jürgen Wegener

J Nazi architecture: The house of German Art in Munich, designed by Hitler's favourite architect, Paul Troost

K Nazi Spectacle: The Dietrich Eckart open-air theatre, used for Nazi ceremonies

**L The Führer Myth: Herman Hoyer's painting of Hitler speaking
to his early followers, exhibited in 1937**

Questions

1 What do Sources A and B tell us about the cultural and propaganda concerns of the Nazi authorities? **(8 marks)**

2 Using your own knowledge, explain the extent to which Source C was typical of Nazi philosophy. **(4 marks)**

3 Why did the Nazis object to the jokes in Source D? **(5 marks)**

4 Identify the cultural messages being conveyed in Sources E–L. **(10 marks)**

5 Hitler declared, 'In this world human culture and civilization are inseparably bound up with the existence of the Aryan.' To what extent do these Sources reflect this belief? **(10 marks)**

9 SOCIAL POLICY

Nazi social policy revealed a mass of contradictions which were never resolved and in some cases were probably incapable of resolution. This paradox reflected the evolution of the Nazi movement's ideology as a hotch-potch of ideas and the fact that Nazism meant different things to different people even within the movement itself. For example, the appeal of Nazism to peasants and the lower middle classes, artisans and professional people, implied a hostility to large-scale capitalism which did not fit easily with Hitler's rearmament programme and the desire for co-operation with German industrialists. An even more glaring contradiction was the insistence of the Nazis on the unified Germanic community of equals, at the same time as the deliberate Nazi curtailment of any serious attempts at female emancipation, on the insistence that the woman's place was in the home and her prime duty was to produce sons for the Reich. In many instances women were positively forced out of full-time occupations.

The Nazis did practise specific forms of social engineering. For example, organisations like the Labour Front and Hitler Youth might be seen as genuine attempts to mould a 'Folk Community' which would overcome traditional class differences and weld together those lucky enough to be classified as true Aryan members of the master race.

The impact of these policies varied. For example, attempts to exacerbate anti-semitic feelings among the German population met with mixed success except where the groundwork had already been done. The history of Nazi Germany shows that totalitarian states can attempt social engineering, but without clear objectives and careful indoctrination over a long period, success is not guaranteed.

A Hitler On Women

(i) The slogan 'Emancipation of Women' was invented by Jewish intellectuals and its content was formed by the same spirit. In the really good times of German life the German woman had no need to emancipate herself. . .

If the man's world is said to be the State, his struggle, his readiness to devote his powers to the service of the community, then it may perhaps be said that the woman's is a smaller world. For her world is her husband, her family, her children, and her home. . . The two worlds are not antagonistic. They complement each other, they belong together just as man and woman belong together.

We do not consider it correct for the woman to interfere in the world of the man, in his main sphere. We consider it natural if these two worlds remain distinct. . .

The sacrifices which the man makes in the struggle of his nation, the woman makes in the preservation of that nation in individual cases. What the man gives in courage on the battlefield, the woman gives in eternal self-sacrifice, in eternal pain and suffering. Every child that a woman brings into the world is a battle, a battle waged for the existence of her people.

From Hitler's 'Address to Women' at the Nuremberg Party Rally, 8 September 1934

(ii) I detest women who dabble in politics. And if their dabbling extends to military matters, it becomes utterly unendurable. In no local section of the Party has a woman ever had the right to hold even the smallest post. It has therefore often been said that we were a party of misogynists, who regarded a woman only as a machine for making children, or else as a plaything. That's far from being the case. I attached a lot of importance to women in the field of the training of youth, and that of good works. . . Everything that entails combat is exclusively men's business. There are so many other fields in which one must rely upon women. Organising a house, for example.

Hitler speaking on 26 January 1942, from *Hitler's Table-Talk* (1988)

B The Function of Women
(i) Beyond the bounds of perhaps otherwise necessary bourgeois law and usage, and outside the sphere of marriage, it will be the sublime task of German women and girls of good blood, acting not frivolously but from a profound moral seriousness, to become mothers to children of soldiers setting off to battle, of whom destiny alone knows if they will return or die for Germany.

From an order by Himmler to the SS

(ii) The parents of girls enrolled in the German Girls' League have filed a complaint with the wardship court at Habel-Brandenburg concerning leaders of the League who have intimated to their daughters that they should bear illegitimate children; these leaders have pointed out that in view of the prevailing shortage of men, not every girl could expect to get a husband in future, and that the girls should at least fulfil their task as German women and donate a child to the Führer.

From a report to the Ministry of Justice, 1944

C Population Policy

Anyone who has a hereditary illness can be rendered sterile by a surgical operation if, according to the experience of medical science, there is a strong probability that his/her offspring will suffer from serious hereditary defects of a physical or mental nature . . . it is not only the decline in population which is the cause of serious concern but equally the increasingly evident genetic make-up of our people. Whereas the hereditarily healthy families have for the most part adopted a policy of having only one or two children, countless numbers of inferiors and those suffering from hereditary ailments are reproducing unrestrainedly while their sick and asocial offspring are a burden on the community.

From the 'Law For The Prevention Of Hereditarily Diseased Offspring', 14 July 1933

D Rules For Marriage

1 Remember that you are a German.
2 If you are genetically healthy you should not remain unmarried.
3 Keep your body pure.
4 You should keep your mind and spirit pure.
5 As a German choose only a spouse of the same or Nordic blood.
6 In choosing a spouse, ask about his ancestors.
7 Health is also a precondition for physical beauty.
8 Marry only for love.
9 Don't look for a playmate but for a companion for marriage.
10 You should want to have as many children as possible.

'Ten Commandments For The Choice Of A Spouse' (1934)

E Nazism and Christianity

(i) The Christian spirit and the 'dirty Jewish' spirit must be separated. A sharp cut must be made to divide the Bible into what is Christian and what is anti-Christian.

From A. Rosenberg: *The Role of the Jews in the Conduct of the Times* (1920)

(ii) National Socialist and Christian concepts are irreconcilable. The Christian churches build upon man's ignorance, and are endeavouring to keep the greatest possible number of people in a state of ignorance. . . National Socialism, on the other hand, rests on scientific foundations. . . We National Socialists . . . demand of ourselves that we live as naturally as possible, that is to say in accord with the laws of life. . .

The consequence of the irreconcilability between National Socialist and Christian views is that we must refuse to strengthen existing Christian denominations or to sponsor new ones. It was for this reason that the idea of establishing a Protestant National Church by merging the various Evangelical churches was ultimately rejected, since the Protestant Church is just as hostile to us as the Catholic Church. . . All influences which might impair, or even harm, the leadership exercised by the Führer with the aid of the National Socialist Party must be eliminated. . . Only when that has happened will the nation's leadership exercise its full influence over the individual citizen.

From a document written by Martin Bormann, 7 July 1941

Questions

1 Explain the concern of the Nazis with population policy as expressed in the final paragraph of Source A (i) and Source B (ii). **(5 marks)**

2 Compare and contrast Nazi views on the role of women as expressed in Sources A and B. **(6 marks)**

3 Using your own knowledge, assess the extent to which Nazi attitudes towards women as reflected in Sources A and B were carried out in practice. **(8 marks)**

4 Explain the relationship between Sources C and D and Nazi racial policies. **(7 marks)**

5 Use Source E, and your own knowledge, to explain the Nazi concern with the Churches in Germany. **(7 marks)**

6 Assess the validity of the statement that 'The Third Reich did partly instigate and partly accelerate developments towards greater social equality, or at least upward mobility.' **(10 marks)**

10 THE ARMY AND REARMAMENT

The army had long enjoyed an honoured and privileged position in Germany, and the humiliation of its enforced reduction under the Treaty of Versailles had been much resented and proved hard to bear. Many of the generals, representative of the old German conservative tradition and hostile to the radicalism of the new Nazi right, did not welcome the Nazi accession to power. Nevertheless, the army was relieved by the elimination of Röhm and the threat from the SA in 1934, and the reintroduction of conscription in 1935 was widely welcomed.

The army and the Nazi Party remained essentially distinct and separate after the Röhm Purge, despite the oath of loyalty to Hitler. In fact, this situation continued even after the re-organisation of 1938 which saw the removals of the War Minister and Commander-in-Chief, and Hitler's elevation to Minister of War. The army was not untouched by events in Germany – the social composition of the officer corps was widened for example – but, nevertheless, its professionalism and prestige remained in good order. Hitler needed a professional army to fulfil his aims in foreign policy.

There was limited resistance to Hitler from within the army in 1938 when it seemed that he was about to involve Germany in war. However, the Chief of General staff, General Beck, failed to persuade other army leaders to overthrow Hitler. Even when Hitler's assumption of the role of Commander-in-Chief in 1941 signalled his triumph over the officer corps, there was no active resistance.

Opposition from the army re-surfaced in the Bomb Plot of 1944 – the generals involved wished to save Germany from military catastrophe – but even at that stage many of the generals failed to act decisively. July 1944 marked the end of any form of military resistance to Hitler. The army had accepted Hitler as Head of State and implicated itself in the Röhm Purge of 1934. Its integrity was compromised and, despite gaining from the rearmament programme, the ultimate price was paid at the end of the war when the General Staff was dissolved by the Allies.

A The New Military Oath
I swear by God this holy oath, that I will render to Adolf Hitler, Leader of the German nation and people, Supreme Commander of the

Armed Forces, unconditional obedience, and I am ready as a brave soldier to risk my life at any time for this oath.

Military Oath introduced August 1934

B The Armed Forces and the State

With the introduction of general conscription, the Armed Forces again become the great school of national education. . . The Führer designates the completion of military service as the prerequisite for the granting of the rights of citizenship. Service in the Armed Forces is therefore the last and highest step in the course of the general education of a young German, from parental home, through school, Hitler Youth, and the Labour Service. The educational goal of the Wehrmacht is not only the basically trained soldier and the master of a weapon, but also the man who is aware of his nationality and of his general duties towards the State. . . The Wehrmacht does not need to pursue prestige politics. Its best propaganda is the successful education of the youth in the spirit of National-Socialism, according to the will of its supreme Commander.

From a decree by Minister of Defence General Blomberg, 16 April 1935

C Political Instruction in the Army

The officer corps of the Wehrmacht can only fulfil its task of leadership in the nation and State if it adopts the National Socialist ideology which gives direction to the life of the German nation and State and appropriates it intellectually totally and with conviction. Thus, I consider the uniform political education and instruction of the officer corps of all three sections of the Wehrmacht to be particularly important.

From a directive by Blomberg, 30 January 1936

D General Von Fritsch Looks Back

On 3 January 1934, I was appointed Commander-in-Chief with effect from 1 February against the Führer's wishes, against Blomberg's wishes, but under the strongest pressure from Field Marshal von Hindenburg.

I found a heap of ruins, in particular a severe crisis of confidence within the High Command.

Reichenau's and the Party's struggle against me began on the day of my appointment in so far as it had not already begun. . .

The Party sees in me not only the man who opposed the ambitions of the SA but also the man who tried to block the influx of party-political maxims into the army.

Apart from the fact that the basis of our present army is National

Socialist and must be so, the infiltration of party-political influences into the army cannot be tolerated since such influences can lead only to fragmentation and dissolution. . .

Reichenau's machinations meant that my relationship with Blomberg was continually troubled. Throughout these years I never succeeded in establishing a relationship with Blomberg based on trust as should have been the case. . .

In the autumn of 1934, there was great agitation as a result of the machinations of the SS. The SS maintained the army was preparing a *putsch*, and reports came in from all the military districts that the SS was planning a big coup. . . The Führer made a speech which was a clear statement of loyalty to the army and its leader. After the Führer's speech, the SS agitation decreased somewhat. But from the summer of 1935 it increased again . . . there was hardly a single senior officer who did not feel that the SS were spying on him. . .

Finally, the SS military wing, which is continually being expanded, must create conflict with the army through its very existence. It is the living proof of mistrust towards the army and its leadership.

Taken from an account written by Chief of the Army Leadership, General von Fritsch, two days before his enforced resignation on 3 February 1938. (Reichenau was Blomberg's Chief of Staff at the Defence Ministry)

E Rearmament
Growth in size of the German army

Unit	1933	1934	1935	1936	1937	1938	1939 (Peace)	1939 (War)
Army Group H.Q.	2	2	3	3	4	6	6	11
Corps H.Q.	–	10	10	12	13	19	22	26
Division H.Q.	10	24	29	39	39	51	51	102
Battalions:								
Infantry	84	166	287	334	352	476	476	906
Artillery	24	95	116	148	187	228	228	482
Panzer	–	6	12	16	24	34	34	34

Statistics from German sources

F Military Dissension
There was no doubt that an attack on Czechoslovakia would bring France and Britain into the conflict at once, thus causing a European or World War. The outcome of such a war would be a general catastrophe for Germany, not only a military defeat.

The German people did not want this war, the purpose of which they did not understand. Similar thoughts were also abroad within the army. . .

History will burden these leaders (the army leaders) with blood guilt if they do not act in accord with their specialised political knowledge and conscience.

From a memorandum by Chief of General Staff Beck, shortly before his resignation in August 1938

Questions

1 Using your own knowledge, explain the significance of the new military oath (Source A), and the circumstances in which it was issued.

(5 marks)

2 Summarise Blomberg's views on the role of the Armed Forces in Nazi Germany, as outlined in Sources B and C. **(7 marks)**

3 What conclusions about the pace of German rearmament can be drawn from Source E? **(5 marks)**

4 How might an historian assess the reliability of Source E? **(4 marks)**

5 Using your own knowledge and Sources D and F, summarise the complaints of Fritsch and Beck and explain the circumstances of their resignations. **(9 marks)**

6 Select any one of Sources A–F and assess its uses and limitations to an historian of army-state relations in the Third Reich. **(5 marks)**

11 THE SS STATE

The SS had its origins in the 'Headquarters Guard' established by Hitler in the 1920s for special tasks 'of a police nature' which could not be entrusted to the more unruly SA. The SS came into its own after the Purge of 1934, as an instrument entirely independent of the State administration and designed to carry out those tasks in which Hitler was particularly interested.

Himmler was *Reichsführer* SS and Chief of the German Police. He controlled the Gestapo (Secret State Police) and by 1937 integration of the SS and the Police was well under way.

Yet another aspect of the SS was the formation of Waffen-SS units, military formations which owed direct allegiance to Hitler. The Waffen SS played a major role in several campaigns of the War. The SS regarded itself as having a European, not just a German, mission – hence the recruitment of Aryan volunteers from other countries into its ranks.

The first concentration camp was established at Dachau in 1933, to house political opponents of the Nazis. After the 1934 Röhm Purge, the SS took over from the SA the running of many camps, which were increasingly used to incarcerate 'anti-social' elements like Jehovah's Witnesses and habitual criminals. By 1938 the camps had become places of forced labour, and during the War they also witnessed summary executions.

Under Himmler the SS insinuated its influence into most aspects of German life, not only through its coercive role, but also through its control of some industrial enterprises, and through its activities in foreign policy and the military sphere. The SS empire came into conflict with institutions like the Foreign Office and even the Nazi Party itself. This may well have suited Hitler: he often avoided difficult decisions and allowed individuals and institutions to fight battles among themselves, which paradoxically increased his own manipulative powers.

Whatever the arguments about the degree to which the Third Reich depended on coercion or popular support for its survival, it cannot be doubted that the institutions of the SS played an important part in creating an atmosphere of general uncertainty and suspicion. Its role was somewhere between Himmler's conception of an elite order on Jesuit lines and Heydrich's description (applied to the Gestapo) of a 'cross between a general maid, and the dustbin of the Reich.'

A The Ethos of the SS

The first principle for us was and is the recognition of the values of blood and selection. . .

We went about it like a seedsman who, wanting to improve the strain of a good old variety which has become crossbred and lost its vigour, goes through the fields to pick the seeds of the best plants. We sorted out the people who we thought unsuitable for the formation of the SS simply on the basis of outward appearance. . .

The second principle and virtue which we tried to instil in the SS, and to give to it as an indelible characteristic for the future, is the will to freedom and a fighting spirit. . .

The third principle and virtue are the concepts of loyalty and honour. . .

The fourth principle and virtue that is valid for us is obedience, which does not hesitate for a moment but unconditionally follows every order which comes from the Führer or is legitimately given by a superior. . .

We shall unremittingly fulfil our task of being the guarantors of Germany's internal security, just as the German *Wehrmacht* guarantees the security of the honour, the greatness, and the peace of the Reich externally. We shall ensure that never again will the Jewish-Bolshevist revolution of sub-humanity be unleashed in Germany, the heart of Europe, either from within or by emissaries from without.

From a speech by Himmler, 12 November 1935

B Himmler's Task for the SS

In a future war we shall not only have the Army's front on land, the Navy's front at sea and the Air Force's front in the skies over Germany, but we shall have a fourth theatre of war: the home front! There are the grass roots which we must keep healthy by hook or by crook because otherwise the three others, the fighting parts of Germany, would once more be stabbed in the back.

We must be clear about the fact that our opponent in this war is not only an opponent in a military sense, but also an ideological opponent . . . our natural enemy, international Bolshevism, led by Jews and Freemasons.

From a lecture by Himmler to *Wehrmacht* Officers, January 1937

C The Concentration Camps

Tolerance means weakness. In the light of this conception, punishment will be mercilessly handed out whenever the interests of the fatherland warrant it. The fellow countryman who is decent but misled will never be affected by these regualtions. But let it be a warning both to the inciting politicians and to intellectual agitators, no matter which: watch out that you are not caught, for otherwise it will be your neck and you will be dealt with according to your own methods. . .

The following offenders, considered as agitators, will be hanged. Anyone who, for the purpose of agitating, does the following in the camp, at work, in the sleeping quarters, in the kitchens and workshops, toilets and places of rest: discusses politics, carries on controversial talks and meetings, forms cliques, loiters around with others; who, for the purpose of supplying the propaganda of the opposition with atrocity stories, collects true or false information about the concentration camp; receives such information, buries it, talks about it to others, smuggles it out of the camp into the hands of foreign visitors or others by clandestine or other means. . .

Anyone who physically attacks a guard or SS man, refuses obedience or declines to work at his place of work, encourages or induces others to do the same for the purposes of mutiny, leaves a marching column or a place of work, howls, shouts, agitates, or holds speeches on the march or during work will be shot on the spot as a mutineer or subsequently hanged.

From the Regulations for Dachau Concentration Camp, issued 1 October 1933, and extended to all camps on 1 August 1934

D Gestapo Activity
A list must be sent in by return of post of those people in your area who were prominent in opposing and slandering the National Socialist movement before the take-over of power. The following details are requested . . . the first name and surname, the date and place of birth, whether or not a Jew, present domicile, profession including all offices held by the person concerned. . . At the same time, a detailed report must be made about the incidents in which the individual was involved, particularly hostile activity towards the NSDAP.

From a message sent to Gestapo offices, Berlin, 22 April 1936

E The Role of the SS in the Occupied Territories
One basic principle must be the absolute rule for the SS man: we must be honest, decent, loyal, and comradely to members of our own blood and to nobody else. What happens to a Russian or to a Czech does not interest me in the slightest. What the nations can offer in the way of good blood of our type we will take, if necessary by kidnapping their children and raising them here with us. Whether nations live in prosperity or kick the bucket interests me only in so far as we need them as slaves for our Culture. . . Whether 10,000

Russian females fall down from exhaustion while digging an anti-tank ditch interests me only in so far as the anti-tank ditch for Germany is finished. . .

If the peace is a final one, we shall be able to tackle our great work of the future. We shall colonize. We shall indoctrinate our boys with the laws of the SS . . . it must be a matter of course that we have children. It must be a matter of course that the most copious breeding should be from this racial elite of the German people. In twenty to thirty years we must really be able to provide the whole of Europe with its ruling class. . .

Today I have asked the Führer that the SS, if we have fulfilled our task and our duty by the end of the war, should have the privilege of holding Germany's most easterly frontier as a defence frontier. . . We shall impose our laws on the east. We shall charge ahead and push our way forward little by little to the Urals. I hope that our generation will successfully bring it about that every age-group has fought in the east, and that every one of our divisions spends a winter in the east every second or third year. Then we shall never grow soft. . . Thus we will create the necessary conditions for the whole Germanic people: to be able, in generations to come, to stand the test in her battles of destiny against Asia, which will certainly break out again.

From a speech by Himmler to SS Leaders in Posen, 4 October 1943

Questions

1 Using your own knowledge, explain how and why the SS had come into prominence by 1936. **(6 marks)**

2 Compare and contrast Sources A, B and E in their views on the role of the SS. **(9 marks)**

3 Use Source C and your own knowledge to explain the role of the concentration camps in Nazi Germany. **(6 marks)**

4 Use Source D and your own knowledge to explain the role of the Gestapo in Nazi Germany. **(6 marks)**

5 Is it possible from Sources A–E to agree with the description of the Third Reich as an 'SS State'? **(8 marks)**

12 OPPOSITION

A combination of censorship and terror makes it difficult to ascertain exactly how much discontent with the Nazi regime existed amongst the German population. There were occasional public manifestations like the Bomb Plot of July 1944, but often alienation from the regime took less overt forms. One must distinguish between opposition to Hitler and opposition to his regime: Hitler's popularity was often greater than that of the Party, because he was seen by many Germans as a national leader. Furthermore, Goebbels' carefully-nurtured Hitler myth allowed the 'ignorant' Führer to escape criticism often levelled at his underlings, whilst he basked in foreign policy successes, at least until 1939.

Nazi and anti-Nazi reports do, however, reveal discontent amongst sections of the population (for example the lower middle class and even some of the peasantry) because of the perceived failure of the Nazis to protect their interests seriously. Moreover, there were grumblings about food shortages and high prices in the mid 1930s. There were also many reports of working class apathy or hostility towards the regime, based on resentment at low wages or the political opposition of Socialist or Communist groups.

Opposition was also provoked by anti-Church measures, such as the attempts to remove crucifixes from churches in Catholic provinces; and there were many protests by Christians against the Euthanasia programme which the Nazis attempted to implement in 1941.

However much discontent may have existed just below the surface in Nazi Germany, the regime was never seriously threatened, probably because different groups had different interests and it was difficult to channel discontent effectively in a one-party police state. Probably the army, alone, possessed the power to threaten the regime after 1934, but many of its leaders were trapped by their oath of loyalty to Hitler, and the discontent of Generals was frequently dumbfounded by Hitler's diplomatic triumphs and military victories in the early stages of the War. The efforts of Conservative generals to overthrow Hitler became concentrated in the latter stages of the War when it seemed that Germany's only salvation lay in the physical elimination of Hitler; but until 1944 there had scarcely been a sustained campaign against Nazi rule.

Historians argue about the precise strengths of opposition elements within Germany. However, it seems that, despite the failure of the regime to win the hearts of the entire population, it was not in serious danger of being overthrown from within, even if the degree of repression had to be increased in proportion to Germany's declining military fortunes and an increasingly 'negative' attitude by the population as a whole.

A Attitudes in a German Town in 1935

The former Communists, especially in Northeim, were as active in opposing the regime as ever, despite repeated arrests, and had even established contact with dissident Nazis. The former SPD members were constantly undermining the regime through word-of-mouth propaganda. The Nazi Party's own members, or at least the 'old fighters,' were very dissatisfied with the way the party had lost its 'true spirit.' Ordinary people were hoping for a purge to rid the party of its disreputable members. Many people noted the contemptuous attitude toward the party expressed by Army officers.

The next month's Gestapo report was even gloomier. Protestants were secretly circulating anti-Nazi writings; the Catholic Church was systematically and ceaselessly trying to make its followers anti-Nazi. The lower classes were ripe for recruitment by the workers' underground. Ex-Social Democrats were hanging together and mutually reinforcing their opposition to the regime. People were still shopping in Jewish stores. Former conservatives were disgusted with the party and were seeking contacts with Army officers. Parents were turning against the Hitler Youth. And the old Nazis felt that they had been bypassed while the new members incessantly complained that too much was being demanded of them.

From Gestapo reports described in W. Allen: *The Nazi Seizure Of Power* (1984)

B More Attitudes Towards the Regime

The reduction in the standard of food is being widely felt, but, although rearmament is mainly to blame, according to his observations, there is no bitterness towards the Army or even towards the officers who enjoy much more sympathy among the general population than in the old days. The two year military service was an unpleasant surprise, but he does not believe that large numbers of people are basically against general military service; it is welcomed on educational grounds even by many Social Democrats. He does not believe the National Socialist mood has penetrated very deeply. However, Hitler has understood how to appeal to nationalist instincts and emotional needs which were already there before. Even the workers have become more nationalist. . .

Hitler is still outside the line of fire of criticism, generally speaking at least, but the messianic belief in him has more or less died out.

People do not criticise him, whereas, for example, Goebbels is almost universally loathed even among the Nazis. . . The reduction in unemployment, rearmament, and the drive it shows in its foreign policy are the big points in favour of Hitler's policy and, on the basis of his own observations, he personally feels that only a tenth of the population does not recognise these facts. People feel that the previous governments were weak-willed and the parties as well. . . Hitler knew how to handle the popular mood and continually to win over the masses. No previous Reich Chancellor had understood anything of that.

From an account by a Jewish teacher to an SPD member, reported by the Social Democratic Party in Exile, 1936

C Communist and Socialist Opposition to the Nazis
Whereas until 1936 the main propaganda emphasis was on distributing lots of pamphlets, at the beginning of 1936 they (the Communists) switched to propaganda by word of mouth, setting up bases in factories and advocated the so-called Popular Front on the French pattern. . .

It became apparent that the Communist propaganda described above was already having some success in various factories. After factory meetings at which speakers of the Labour Front had spoken, some of whom were in fact rather clumsy in their statements, the mood of discontent among the workers was apparent in subsequent discussions . . . the shifting about of workers within the various factories, necessitated by the scarceness of raw materials, creates more fertile soil for the subversion of the workers by the KPD. . .

In the period covered by the report the SPD has worked mainly by means of the dissemination of news . . . (and) the setting up of cells in factories, sports clubs and other organisations. Since the former SPD members carry on propaganda only by word of mouth, it is very difficult to get hold of proof of their illegal activities which would be usable in court. . .

In 1938 we will have to devote particular attention to illegal activity in the factories. Trusted agents have been infiltrated into several big factories in my district who have already provided proof that the KPD and the SPD are carrying out conspiratorial work jointly.

From a Gestapo report from Dusseldorf, 1937

D A Foreigner's Opinion
I have just returned from a visit to Germany. . . There is for the first time since the War a general sense of security. The people are more cheerful. There is a greater sense of general gaiety of spirit throughout the land. It is a happier Germany. . .

As to his (Hitler's) popularity, especially among the youth of Germany, there can be no manner of doubt. The old trust him; the young idolise him. It is not the admiration accorded to a popular leader. It is the worship of a national hero who has saved his country from utter despondency and degradation.

It is true that public criticism of the Government is forbidden in every form. That does not mean that criticism is absent. I have heard the speeches of prominent Nazi orators freely condemned.

But not a word of criticism or of disapproval have I heard of Hitler. . .

To those who have not actually seen and sensed the way Hitler reigns over the heart and mind of Germany this description may appear extravagant. All the same, it is the bare truth. This great people will work better, sacrifice more, and, if necessary, fight with greater resolution because Hitler asks them to do so. . .

On the other hand, those who imagine that Germany has swung back to its old Imperialist temper cannot have any understanding of the character of the change. The idea of a Germany intimidating Europe with a threat that its irresistible army might march across frontiers forms no part of the new vision.

From Lloyd George's article, 'I Talked to Hitler' in *Daily Express*, November 17, 1936

E Youthful Resistance to the Regime

The day of reckoning has come, the day when German youth will settle accounts with the vilest tyranny ever endured by our nation. In the name of German youth, we demand from Adolf Hitler's state the restoration of personal freedom, a German's most precious possession, which it took from us by base deceit.

We grew up in a state where every free expression of opinion has been ruthlessly suppressed. Hitler Youth, storm troops, and SS have tried, in the most receptive years of our lives, to regiment, to revolutionise, and to narcotise us. 'Ideological education' was the name for this despicable method of suffocating budding independent thought in a fog of empty phrases. . .

There can be but one word of action for us: Fight the party! Quit the party organisations, where all discussion is now being stifled. . . Each of us must join in the fight for our future, for a life in freedom and honour in a state that is aware of its moral obligations. . . Students! The eyes of the German nation are upon us. Germany expects from us, from the might of the spirit, the destruction of the National Socialist terror in 1943 . . . the dead of Stalingrad implore us:

'Act, then, my nation, see the beacons' blaze!'

Our nation shall rise against the enslavement of Europe by National Socialism in a new, true burst of freedom and honour.

From a pamphlet distributed by the White Rose group, Munich, February 18, 1943

F Clerical Opposition

'Justice is the state's foundation.' We lament, we regard with great concern, the evidence of how this foundation is being shaken today, how justice – that natural and Christian virtue, which is indispensable to the orderly existence of every human society – is plainly not being implemented and maintained for all. . .

The regular courts have no say over the jurisdiction by decree of the Secret Police. Since none of us know of a way that might give us an impartial control over the measures of the Gestapo – its expulsions, its arrests, its imprisonment of fellow Germans in concentration camps – large groups of Germans have a feeling of being without rights, and what is worse, harbour feelings of cowardly fear. . .

The obligation of my episcopal office to defend the moral order, and the loyalty to my oath, which I swore before God and the government's representative, to prevent to the best of my ability any harm that might come to the German body politic, impel me, in view of the Gestapo's actions, to say this publicly.

From a sermon by Cardinal Count Galen, July 13 1941

G Conservative Opposition

Germans:

Monstrous things have taken place under our eyes in the years past. Against the advice of his experts, Hitler has unscrupulously sacrificed whole armies for his desire for glory, his presumption of power, his blasphemous delusion of being the chosen and inspired instrument of what he calls 'providence'. . . To maintain his power, he has established an unbridled reign of terror, destroying justice, banishing decency, mocking the divine commands of pure humanity, and destroying the happiness of millions. . .

We must not continue on that course! . . . Having examined our conscience before God, we have assumed executive power. Our brave armed forces will guarantee security and order. The police will do their duty. . .

Without hatred, we will attempt the act of domestic conciliation. With dignity, we will attempt that of foreign conciliation. Our first task will be to purge the war of its debasements, and to put a stop to the disastrous destruction of human life, and of cultural and economic treasure behind the fronts.

From General Beck's appeal to the German People, drawn up before the Bomb Plot of July 20 1944

Questions

1 Use Sources A and B to assess the degree to which the Nazis had succeeded in winning over the hearts and minds of the German people by the mid 1930s. **(8 marks)**

2 Which Reports – Gestapo or SPD – are likely to be of most use to historians investigating attitudes towards the Nazi regime? You should refer to the Sources in your answer. **(7 marks)**

3 To what extent does Source C suggest that Left wing opposition within Germany was a serious threat to the Nazis? **(6 marks)**

4 Is the attitude displayed towards the Nazi regime in Source D supported by the evidence of Sources A, B and C? How do you account for any differences? **(8 marks)**

5 Compare and contrast the attitudes towards the Nazi regime displayed in Sources E, F and G. **(9 marks)**

6 Using your own knowledge, explain the circumstances in which General Beck prepared his appeal (Source G). **(3 marks)**

7 Using your own knowledge, and the evidence of Sources A to G, assess the degree to which opposition and resistance to the Nazis from within Germany came predominantly from the Left or the Right. **(10 marks)**

13 FOREIGN POLICY

Few historians would deny that Hitler's expansionist foreign policy was a prime cause of the Second World War and the ultimate destruction of the Third Reich, but there has long been a debate as to the precise nature of Hitler's aims. Some of the earlier analysts of the Third Reich took the line that Hitler was obsessed by a fundamental lust for power which could not be satiated by achieving power in Germany alone, but carried him forward into the realms of virtually unlimited expansion in Europe and even the world. Other historians have carefully investigated Hitler's recorded statements, such as those in *Mein Kampf*, which could be interpreted as demonstrations of a more systematic and limited set of objectives: the abolition of the territorial clauses of the Treaty of Versailles; the unification of all German-speaking peoples into a great Reich; and the establishment of a German empire in Eastern Europe.

Later some revisionist historians, notably A.J.P. Taylor, argued that Hitler's foreign policy was basically a logical extension of that of earlier German leaders, and that Hitler was as much a reactor to the foreign policies of other powers as an initiator of events in his own right.

Some historians have attempted to resolve the controversy by developing the thesis, hardly original when applied to most dynamic leaders, that Hitler combined certain long-term goals (for example 'Lebensraum' in Eastern Europe) with a short-term opportunism (for example the Nazi–Soviet Pact), which freed Hitler from the immediate danger of a two-front war. The debate as to whether Hitler really wanted war at all has perhaps become somewhat sterile, since his approach to foreign policy made it likely that, whatever the gains he was able to make by taking advantage of the appeasement policies and lack of determination on the part of other powers to unite against him, eventually some sort of armed clash would result. It is, of course, possible to argue that for most of the 1930s Hitler pursued an intelligible, and to a large extent successful, foreign policy, but that having become involved in war in 1939 and then having become intoxicated by early military successes, his intuition and relative caution deserted him, leading him to embark on over-ambitious, and in some cases almost suicidal, ventures, such as the declaration of war against the United States.

A Hitler's Early Views on Foreign Policy

The foreign policy of a folkish state must first of all bear in mind the obligation to secure the existence of the race incorporated in this state. This must be done by establishing a healthy and natural relationship between the number and growth of the population, on the one hand, and the extent and quality of its soil on the other. . . Only a sufficiently large space on this earth can ensure the independent existence of a nation. . .

Germany today is not a world power. . . The National Socialist movement must seek to eliminate the present disastrous imbalance between our population and the area of our national territory, regarding the latter as the source of our food and the basis of our political power. And it ought to strive to eliminate the contrast between our past history and the hopelessness of our present political impotence. . .

The demand for the restoration of the frontiers of 1914 is a political absurdity of such proportions and implications as to make it appear a crime. Apart from anything else, the Reich's frontiers in 1914 were anything but logical. In reality they were neither final in the sense of embracing all ethnic Germans, nor sensible with regard to geo-military considerations. . . We are putting an end to the perpetual German march towards the south and west of Europe and turning our eyes towards the land in the east. We are finally putting a stop to the colonial and trade policy of the pre-war period and passing over to the territorial policy of the future.

However, when we speak of new land in Europe today we must principally bear in mind Russia and the border states subject to her. Destiny itself seems to wish to point the way for us here. . . The colossal empire in the East is ripe for dissolution. . .

If we look round for European allies from this point of view, only two states remain: England and Italy . . . whose most natural selfish interests are not, at any rate essentially, opposed to the German people's requirements for existence and are indeed to some extent identified with them.

From A. Hitler: *Mein Kampf* (1925)

B Further Thoughts of Hitler

. . . in contrast to our present statesmen I see Germany's tasks for the future as follows:

1 Overcoming Marxism and its consequences until they have been completely exterminated. The creation of a new unity of mind and will for our people.

2 A general intellectual and moral rearmament of the nation on the basis of this new ideological unity.

3 Technical rearmament.
4 The organisational mobilisation of the national resources for the
purpose of national defence.
5 Once this has been achieved, the securing of the legal recognition
of the new situation by the rest of the world.

From a letter from Hitler to Colonel von Reichenau, 4 December 1932

C The Conservatives Set Out Their Views

The goals of German foreign policy are set first and foremost by the
Versailles treaty. The revision of this treaty – Germany's most pressing
concern – absorbs most of its available energies. . .

The main goal of the territorial revision remains the transformation
of the Eastern frontier, whereby we must seek to acquire all the relevant
Polish territories at the same time. . . Danzig poses only one aspect
of the problem of the corridor as far as we are concerned. . .

In Germany's particular situation it is necessary to avoid diplomatic
conflicts for as long as possible until we have become stronger. . .
A period of relative quiet in foreign affairs would allow us to recover
our strength far more effectively than the launching of continual
diplomatic conflicts which cannot lead to success. . .

The essential points would be a close cooperation with England
and Italy, the greatest possible reassurance for the French
government about these questions which particularly interest it (eg
the German defence programme), a good relationship with Russia,
relations with the United States based on trust, and active
participation in all international questions.

From a memorandum prepared by the Foreign Ministry for presentation
to the Cabinet, 7 April 1933

D Hitler's Thinking in 1937

The aim of German policy was to make secure and to preserve the
racial community and to enlarge it. It was therefore a question of
space.

The German racial community comprised over 85 million people
and, by reason of their number and the narrow limits of habitable
space in Europe, it constituted a tightly packed racial core such as
was not to be found in any other country and such as implied the
right to a greater living space than in the case of other peoples. . . If,
then, we accept the security of our food situation as the principal
point at issue, the space needed to ensure it can be sought only in
Europe, not, as in the liberal-capitalist view, in the exploitation of
colonies. . .

German policy had to reckon with two hate-inspired antagonists,
Britain and France, to whom a German colossus in the centre of

Europe was a thorn in the flesh, and both countries were opposed to any further strengthening of Germany's position either in Europe or overseas...

Germany's problem could be solved only by the use of force, and this was never without attendant risk ... there remain still to be answered the questions 'When?' and 'How?' In this matter there were three contingencies to be dealt with:

Contingency 1: Period 1943–5
After this date only a change for the worse, from our point of view, could be expected... Our relative strength would decrease in relation to the rearmament which would by then have been carried out by the rest of the world...

Contingency 2:
If internal strife in France should develop into such a domestic crisis as to absorb the French army completely and render it incapable of use for war against Germany, then the time for action against the Czechs would have come.

Contingency 3:
If France should be so embroiled in war with another State that she could not 'proceed' against Germany.

For the improvement of our politico-military position our first objective, in the event of our being embroiled in war, must be to overthrow Czechoslovakia and Austria simultaneously in order to remove the threat to our flank in any possible operation against the West...

Actually, the Führer believed that almost certainly Britain, and probably France as well, had already tacitly written off the Czechs and were reconciled to the fact that this question would be cleared up in due course by Germany.

Taken from the Hossbach Memorandum, 5 November 1937

E Reflections on the Hossbach Memorandum

Hitler's exposition was in large part day-dreaming, unrelated to what followed in real life. Even if seriously meant, it was not a call to action, at any rate not to the action of a great war; it was a demonstration that a great war would not be necessary. . . The conference was a manoeuvre in domestic affairs . . . (Hitler) had . . . to win them (the Conservatives) for a programme of increased armaments. . . Hitler did not make plans – for world conquest or for anything else. He assumed that others would provide opportunities, and that he would seize them.

A.J.P. Taylor: *The Origins of the Second World War* (1964)

F Hitler Sums Up

When I came to power in 1933 . . . I had to reorganise everything, from the people itself to the armed forces. First came domestic reorganisation, the removal of the symptoms of decay and defeatism, an education to heroism. While engaged in that reorganisation, I dealt with the second task: freeing Germany from its international bonds. . . There followed, in 1935, the reintroduction of universal military service. After that, the remilitarisation of the Rhineland. . . A year later came Austria. That step, too, was considered very risky. It resulted in a major strengthening of the Reich. The next step was Bohemia, Moravia, and Poland. . .

One will reproach me and say: struggle, and struggle again. I see struggle as the fate of all living creatures. No man can escape it, unless he wishes to be defeated. The increasing numbers of our people require a larger amount of space. It was my aim to bring about a more sensible relation between population and space. That must be the struggle's starting point. No nation can escape the solution of that task. If it does, it must degenerate and slowly become extinct. This is the lesson of history.

From a speech by Hitler to Commanders-in-Chief, 23 November 1939

Questions

1 What, according to Hitler in Sources A and B, should be the principles of German foreign policy? **(7 marks)**

2 To what extent did Hitler's foreign policy in the 1930s accord with the views of his Conservative allies in 1933, as outlined in Source C? **(7 marks)**

3 Were Hitler's views on Germany's priorities in 1937 (Source D) the same as those he outlined in 1925 (Source A)? **(6 marks)**

4 Using your own knowledge, and Sources D and E, explain why there has been a controversy amongst historians about Hitler's aims in foreign policy. **(8 marks)**

5 Using only Sources A, B, D and F, assess the degree to which Hitler maintained a consistent line in his views on foreign policy down to 1941. **(9 marks)**

14 PERSONALITIES AND HISTORIOGRAPHY

Some historians of the Third Reich have focused on the personalities of the Nazi leaders, others, particularly in more recent times, have concentrated their analysis on other aspects of the period. It is impossible here to deal with all aspects of either the personalities or the historiography of the Third Reich. There have, however, been many debates. One of the earliest concerned the degree to which Nazism was an 'inevitable' development in German history, with roots in Bismarck's newly unified state in the late nineteenth century. Others have questioned the degree to which Nazism was a product of particular conditions, such as the First World War and the Great Depression. It has also been asked whether Nazism should be seen essentially as a variant of trends apparent in most of Europe after 1918. Did Hitler come to power as head of a mass movement or through the backstairs intrigue of a group of influential Conservatives? Was Fascism the manifestation of the last great crisis of capitalism, as many Marxists at the time believed? Was Nazism an outgrowth of capitalism, or a reaction against the development of a certain type of capitalism? How significant were particular phenomena like anti-Semitism in the rise of Hitler? To what extent did Hitler's regime rest upon mass support, and to what extent coercion or apathy? Why did Germany rather than other advanced industrial nations adopt Fascism as a 'solution' to its problems? Was world war the inevitable consequence of Hitlerism? How specific or unlimited were Hitler's aims in foreign policy?

Debate on these, and other issues, has been influenced by the need felt by many Germans, especially of a later generation, to evaluate their own recent past. The interpretations have also been affected by shifts in post-War attitudes and trends reflecting phenomena such as the Cold War. The following extracts present some interpretations of Hitler's particular place in the debate.

A Bullock on Hitler

The fact that his career ended in failure, and that his defeat was pre-eminently due to his own mistakes, does not by itself detract from Hitler's claim to greatness. The flaw lies deeper. For these remarkable powers were combined with an ugly and strident egotism, a moral and intellectual cretinism. The passions which ruled Hitler's mind were ignoble: hatred, resentment, the lust to dominate, and, where he could not dominate, to destroy. His career did not exalt but debased the human condition, and his twelve years' dictatorship was barren of all ideas save one – the further extension of his own power and that of the nation with which he had identified himself. . .

The great revolutions of the past, whatever their ultimate fate, have been identified with the release of certain powerful ideas: individual conscience, liberty, equality, national freedom, social justice. National Socialism produced nothing. Hitler constantly exalted force over the power of ideas and delighted to prove that men were governed by cupidity, fear, and their baser passions. . .

It is this emptiness, this lack of anything to justify the suffering he caused rather than his own monstrous and ungovernable will which makes Hitler both so repellent and so barren a figure.

From A. Bullock: *Hitler: A Study In Tyranny* (1962)

B Fest on Hitler
The unique mixture and contrast of banality and significance, of the commonplace that yet had historic status, seems one further example of the dialectic and driving mechanism of this dissonant character, which took its most powerful drive from the tension between what he was and what he wished to be. Hitler was undoubtedly great and a figure of historic significance. There is tragedy here too; the tragedy is that of his victims, and the greatness stems almost exclusively from destructiveness. In the sum total of this life, constructive achievements are lacking to an extent scarcely paralleled among the most savage figures of history. What his contemporaries saw as constructive achievements were either counterfeits devised for effect with the aid of compulsion, deception, and propaganda tricks, or were intended solely to give him the means to further his all-embracing destructiveness. . .

To equate the obviously inferior features of Hitler's personality with lack of intelligence or actual stupidity would be to make the same mistake as so many of his self-confident partners and opponents. . . On the basis of a few primitive notions fixed at an early stage in complex aggressive attitudes, he generally reacted with extraordinary acuteness and, to use one of his own favourite expressions, with 'icy coldness', with no counterbalancing sense of compassion, of morality or of respectability – a familiar phenomenon in psychiatry.

From J. Fest: *The Face Of The Third Reich* (1972)

C The 'Hitler Phenomenon'
. . . Concentration on Hitler himself, which is the essence of the biographical method but has also, at times dominated monographic studies, has aroused a certain degree of uneasiness, in so far as it takes too little account of general economic and social conditions

which certainly play a part in explaining what 'made Hitler possible' and why his policy and conduct of the war took the form they did. Especially since the 1960s, a more 'structural' trend in contemporary research has sought to remedy this defect. Nazism has thus been viewed more and more in a transnational and comparative light, as an aspect of 'European fascism'. . . On the other hand, an overemphasis on the structural method, and the acceptance of its results to the exclusion of others, have certainly led to underestimating Hitler's unique and decisive role in the history of the Third Reich and the context of his time, so that he has been too easily considered as 'replaceable' and in some ways even a 'weak dictator'.

From K. Hildebrand: *The Third Reich* (1984)

Questions

1 What problems and controversies can you identify in Sources A–C concerning the importance of Hitler in German and world history?

(8 marks)

2 Assess the contribution of any historian with whom you are familiar to your understanding of *either* a particular problem in the history of the Third Reich *or* the history of Germany generally between 1933 and 1945. **(12 marks)**

15 DEALING WITH EXAMINATION QUESTIONS

Specimen Source Question Answer

(*See pages 47–52*)

1 Using Sources A and B, and your own knowledge, explain the methods by which the Nazis promoted anti-semitic propaganda in Germany during the 1930s. **(8 marks)**

The Nazis promoted anti-semitic propaganda in Germany during the 1930s in a variety of ways. Source A demonstrates the crude approach often employed in Nazi publications. In books produced for children, Jewish physical characteristics were caricatured and contrasted with 'Aryan' types, the intention being to create unpleasant stereotypes and prepare minds to readily accept such measures as the exclusion of Jewish children from schools.

Source B uses a similar approach creating stereotypes. The story of Inge is calculated to inculcate fear, particularly with its imagery of the devil and implications of unsavoury intentions; whilst the positive image of the Nazi (BDM) leader is reinforced.

Similar propaganda was employed by the Nazis in books, journals such as *Der Sturmer*, films and the media generally, and was aimed at all sections of society. Sometimes racism was given a pseudo-scientific justification. The intention was to isolate the Jews, reinforcing measures like the 1933 boycott, and preparing the population for measures involving the exclusion of Jews from public life and the protection of the law.

2 Using your own knowledge, explain the reference to 'Jewish laws' in Source C. **(3 marks)**

The 'Jewish laws' referred to are the Nuremberg Laws promulgated in 1935. These banned marriage and sexual relations between Jews and non-Jews and effectively deprived Jews of citizenship and thereby the protection of the law.

3 Using your own knowledge, explain the references to the 'recent incidents' and 'Jewish pogroms' in Source D. **(4 marks)**

The 'recent incidents' and 'Jewish pogroms' referred to are the events collectively known as 'Crystal Night'. In 1938, following the assassination of a German diplomat in Paris by a young Jew, Jewish synagogues and property throughout Germany were wrecked and thousands of Jews were herded into concentration camps. The pogrom was initiated chiefly by the SS, despite claims that it was spontaneous.

4 To what extent do Sources C and D suggest that anti-semitic propaganda
was effective in influencing the German population?   **(6 marks)**

The evidence of Sources C and D about the effectiveness of anti-semitic
propaganda in influencing the German population is not conclusive. Source
C specifically states that the Jewish laws 'are not taken very seriously' and
are being used as a diversionary tactic to obscure other problems. It is
admitted that some people have been persuaded into 'fanatical' hatred of the
Jews; but claims are also made that the majority of the population go out
of their way to show their opposition to anti-Jewish excesses.

Source D shows conflicting reactions: depending partly on class and
location. It is suggested that areas in which the Jews were well-assimilated
were less likely to be influenced by anti-semitic propaganda.

5 What questions might an historian ask in order to evaluate the reliability
of Sources C and D?   **(4 marks)**

An historian would note that both Sources C and D were reports by
supporters of the banned SDP party – almost certainly with an axe to grind
against the Nazis. But, even assuming that the reports were trying to be
objective, one would ask: were these reports based on hearsay or were they
direct evidence? How was the information obtained? What was the purpose
of the Reports? Was the Report from within Germany (Source C) more reliable
as evidence than that compiled in exile (Source D)?

6 What evidence of propaganda is contained in Sources E and F? **(6 marks)**

Both Sources E and F contain propaganda. Source E shows three of Hitler's
favourite themes: the blaming of any war (which was on the horizon) on
the Jews; the implication that Jews operated as an international conspiracy;
and, not least, the linking of Judaism with Communism.

Source F likewise blames the war, then in progress for two years, on the
Jews; and implies an international conspiracy, with the Jews in influential
positions, pulling the strings in countries which speak out against the Nazis.
For good measure, Goebbels uses emotive words like 'parasitical' and 'fleas'
to denigrate Jews, and he takes the opportunity to propagate Nazi racial
theories.

7 Using your own knowledge, explain the role of Himmler and the SS in the
Final Solution.   **(7 marks)**

Himmler and the SS played a pivotal role in implementing the Final Solution.
Already by the late 1930s the SS controlled the police and concentration
camp system and therefore already had considerable experience of dealing
with Germany's Jews. Himmler then acquired the role of implementing
Nazi racial policies, in particular the Final Solution, from 1942. The SS
played a crucial role in the Wannsee Conference and the arrangements for the
liquidation of Europe's Jews. Many Jews had already been shot in the

occupied territories like Russia. Now the SS were to run extermination camps like Auschwitz, and had the general task of guarding the purity of the Aryan race. In short, Himmler and his SS were effectively responsible for administering the Final Solution throughout Europe.

8 Using only the evidence of Sources A–G, assess the validity of the statement that 'anti-semitism was less of a genuine belief of the Nazis than a convenient weapon to support or excuse their policies.' **(8 marks)**

Examples of anti-semitism abound throughout these Sources. Sources A and B demonstrate anti-semitism in its crudest form. Sources C and D deal only with the impact of anti-semitic propaganda and practices. Sources E and F use the Jews as scapegoats for war, or the threat of war. Source G is an appeal by Himmler to his own SS commanders to be uncompromising in their duty to exterminate a lesser race. It was clearly convenient for the Nazis to use an identification group like the Jews to excuse their involvement in war; and indeed as a scapegoat generally. However, the vehemence of the propaganda, including occasions when Nazi was speaking to Nazi, and, for example, Himmler's insistence on the moral rightness of his policies and the determination of the perpetrators to retain their 'decency' throughout, suggests that anti-semitism was a central part of Nazi policy and a deeply-ingrained belief, not just an opportunistic weapon to promote their own power or other specific ends.

Approaching Essay Questions

The key to writing successful history essays must always be in the last resort the ability to achieve relevance, in other words, you must answer the particular question set. Relevance is worth much more than length or a mass of detail. Accurate knowledge is also important, but only if it is employed to back up a particular argument, not for its own sake. Un-analytical narrative, or prepared answers to a topic which do not meet the requirements of the particular title set, are probably the commonest failings of examination answers. Conversely, the best answers are often concise, always relevant, analytical, and show evidence of wide and thoughtful reading. Your command of the English language is not being tested as such, but you must be able to present your arguments effectively!

Plan your essays. Break the question down into its key components. What are the key phrases or words in the question? Give your essays a shape: an introduction which will introduce the main argument and possibly indicate how you hope to approach it; a logical main body, written in paragraphs (sometimes ignored by students!); and a conclusion which does not repeat the bulk of your essay but neatly draws together the threads. Other issues such as style and use of quotations are also important if you wish to write lucidly and well. As with most things in life, essay writing usually improves with practice.

In most of the history essays you encounter, you will be asked to evaluate a statement or quotation, or answer a direct question. There are usually different approaches you may adopt: therefore, 'model' answers must be treated with caution. It is, for example, quite in order to approach a controversial issue by considering evidence which supports different sides of an argument, without necessarily coming down decisively on one side of a particular interpretation. On the other hand, it is equally acceptable to argue a particular viewpoint, provided you can produce supporting evidence. Credit will usually be given if you show relevant knowledge of contemporary and/or more recent sources.

There are books available which deal in some depth with issues such as analytical reading, question analysis and essay-writing. Students may well find any of the following useful:

C. Brasher: *The Young Historian* (OUP 1970)

J. Cloake, V. Crinnon and S. Harrison: *The Modern History Manual* (Framework Press 1987)

J. Fines: *Studying To Succeed – History at 'A' Level and Beyond* (Longman 1986)

The following list of essay titles on Nazi Germany includes suggestions (no more than suggestions!) on how to approach them; plus a specimen answer. Use them as part of your course or for examination practice.

Possible Essay Titles

1 Was backstairs intrigue or popular support responsible for Hitler's accession to power in 1933?

The key phrases here are obviously 'backstairs intrigue' and 'popular support'. A balanced answer is likely to conclude that both factors were important to Hitler's appointment as Chancellor in January 1933. Students should evaluate the extent to which the Nazi Party *had* won popular backing by 1933 – analysing the election results, the impact of the economic crisis, and factors like Nazi propaganda, which all helped to mobilise support. However, answers should also discuss the role of intrigue amongst non-Nazi politicians in paving Hitler's path to power, and their motives for acting in the way they did.

2 To what extent had the Nazi Party achieved a stranglehold of power over Germany by the end of 1933?

One approach to this question would be to compare the power of the Nazi Party at the beginning of 1933 with that at the end of the year. It should be pointed out that Hitler's accession to the Chancellorship in January 1933 did not immediately transform Germany into a Nazi state. Some discussion of the importance of later measures – for example, the purge of the civil service, the abolition of trade unions, the beginnings of a terror state, the abolition of other parties – is necessary to establish the degree to which the Nazis had permeated German life. Good answers should point out that the Nazi Party itself was not a monolithic organisation, and that even Hitler was not secure in his dictatorial powers until the Röhm Purge of June 1934.

3 Why, and with what consequences, did Hitler defeat the 'Second Revolution' in 1934?

This question clearly concerns the significance of the Röhm Purge of June 1934, and must be dealt with in two parts. Firstly, why did Hitler embark on the Purge? Important factors which should be discussed include Hitler's refusal to implement the more radical policies of some of his supporters; the fears of businessmen and army generals about their future; the somewhat anomalous position of the SA in the Nazi state; and the opportunity for Hitler and his cronies to rid themselves of real or imagined opponents.

The consequences, which should form the second part of the essay, are reasonably straightforward. Students should discuss the changed relationship between Hitler and the Army; the liquidation of Hitler's political enemies; the impact on the SA and SS; and the impact of the Purge on Hitler's own political position and consolidation of power.

4 How valid is the claim that 'the Third Reich was a bedlam of rival hierarchies, competing centres of power and ambiguous chains of command'?

This is a difficult question and the terms of reference need to be clearly defined. Students need to consider various factors: the role of individuals and institutions in Nazi Germany; the role of the Party and the complex issue of its relationship with the state; and the whole issue of Hitler's personal power and method of governing. A good answer should chart the changes in relationships which occurred, for example from the early days of 1933–4 to the later years of the war when Bormann and the Party extended their powers.

5 How important was the Party in the Nazi state?

Answers must show more than just a knowledge of the structure of the Nazi Party, and should attempt some assessment of its role in Germany between 1933 and 1945. There was no one clearly defined role for the Party, although it was expected by Hitler to play a propagandist role in 'leading' the German people. The Party did have the duty of supervising the institutions of the state, but its success in fulfilling this role varied from department to department and was also affected by the personalities of the individuals involved.

6 How valid is the phrase 'the SS State' as a description of the Third Reich?

This question obviously presupposes a knowledge of the structure and functions of the SS. However, beyond that, an analysis of its precise, and changing, role in the Third Reich should be given. A starting point for an answer is likely to be the enhancement of the SS's role as its reward for implementing the 1934 Purge. This could be followed by an analysis of its links with the police and security apparatus; the development of a military role in the Waffen SS; and its crucial role in the administration of Germany's wartime conquests and implementation of Nazi racial policies. A good answer should attempt some assessment of the power and independence of the SS vis-à-vis other institutions.

7 Does Goebbels' career illustrate that there are limits to what even the most brilliant propagandist can achieve?

There are two principal thrusts to this question. Some assessment should be given of the role of Goebbels in the Third Reich (hopefully with some knowledge of his part in the Nazi rise to power before 1933). This should then be followed by an evaluation of the effectiveness of the various forms of propaganda employed by the Nazis, before attempting an overall conclusion.

8 How valid is the statement that Nazi economic policy was 'a series of compromises and contradictions that solved nothing'?

There are several strands to this question. Clearly the basis of Nazi economic policy must be explained; some understanding of Germany's economic problems should be demonstrated; and some overall evaluation of the policy in terms of fulfilment or otherwise of those aims is called for. Key elements are likely to include the impact of public works' schemes, rearmament, the Four Year Plans, trading agreements with other countries, and possibly Nazi policy towards agriculture and business.

9 Assess Nazi policy towards women in the Third Reich.

Answers need to show awareness of the main facets of Nazi policy in this area: the assumption that the woman's primary duty was towards her home, husband and children; the Nazi attempt to limit the steps towards female emancipation which were a feature of Weimar Germany; the change signified by the increasing recruitment of women into the workforce as the needs of the regime were affected in the late 1930s and the war years.

Some attempt to assess the effectiveness of Nazi policies in the context of this contradiction between ideology and practical requirements is also called for.

10 Assess the respective roles of demagogic leadership and terror in the Nazi political system.

See the specimen answer on page 98.

11 'The Church controversy was one of the major unresolved issues of the
   Third Reich.' Why was this so?

This is a straightforward question provided students have enough background
knowledge about both the Protestant and Catholic churches in Germany.
The issue of 'controversy' and instances of co-operation, opposition and
resistance should all be discussed. Why did the Nazis have an ambivalent
attitude towards Christianity? How effective were Nazi attempts to establish
a new Church? Were there any differences between the dealings of the Nazis
with the Protestant and Catholic churches? Why, despite many instances of
dissatisfaction and (generally) individual acts of disobedience, were public
confrontations largely avoided?

12 Did Hitler succeed in his aim of creating a '*Volksgemeinschaft*' (National
   Community)?

This is not an easy question, and requires a good understanding of both the
'community' ideology which underpinned much of Nazi thinking and
propaganda, and how seriously and successfully it was translated into practice
in the Third Reich. Clearly an answer should consider Nazi racial policies,
in the light of the Nazis' emphasis on the purity of the German race. However,
consideration should also be given to their aim of abolishing class distinction
and class consciousness. The degree to which Nazi political, social and
economic policies achieved the aim of creating an integrated community is a
matter of debate, but there is plenty of material available in English on the
reactions of Germans of all classes to Nazi policies.

13 Do you agree that anti-semitism was 'the core of Hitler's system of beliefs
   and the central motivation of his policies'?

There is considerable scope here for a thorough analysis of Nazi policies
towards the Jews. Clearly answers will describe the principal stages in the
implementation of anti-semitic policies, from the boycott and purges of 1933
to the Final Solution of the war years. However, the key phrases are 'core'
and 'motivation'. Students should consider the extent to which the anti-
semitism of the Nazis was basically ideological or opportunistic in origin, or a
combination of both, and indeed, what variations of belief may have existed
amongst the Nazis themselves, since there is evidence that for a considerable
time Hitler refrained from some of the extreme measures canvassed by his
more raucous supporters.

14 Is it possible to speak of a 'cultural revolution' in Germany between 1933
   and 1939?

To attempt this question successfully students need a sound knowledge of the principal themes in German culture in the Third Reich. Taking the word 'culture' in its broadest sense, developments in education as well as the arts generally might be dealt with. Attention should be paid to the aims of Nazi ideologues like Goebbels and Rosenberg, and the extent to which institutions like the Chambers of Arts, Music, and so on, succeeded in imposing a Nazi model on cultural outpourings. Some analysis should also be made of the impact of these policies: to what extent were the cultural lives of the German people transformed? There is considerable evidence on this topic now available.

15 Why was opposition within Germany to the Nazi regime so ineffectual?

It is important to define the term 'opposition' since, for example, there are official reports and 'unofficial' evidence from the Third Reich of considerable disaffection with the regime, demonstrated through grumblings, go-slows at work and so on. However, active resistance, in terms of attempts to topple the regime, is a different proposition, and can be separated into categories such as military, nationalist/conservative, left-wing/communist. The reasons for the failure of this opposition, and acts of resistance (such as the Bomb Plot of 1944) may then be analysed. Hopefully some acquaintance with the historiography of different aspects of the opposition may be demonstrated.

16 Examine the changing nature of the relations between the German army and the Nazi Party during the Third Reich.

A straightforward assignment which should take students through the events of the 1934 Purge, re-armament, the Blomberg-Fritsch affair of 1938, opposition from army generals before and during the war, culminating in the 1944 Plot, and the destruction of the old officer corps. Personal relationships between the Nazi leaders and the army hierarchy may be examined, and possibly relations between the army and the SS.

17 How valid is Alan Bullock's statement that Hitler's foreign policy to 1939 combined 'consistency of aim with complete opportunism in method and tactics'?

Students should discuss (a) Hitler's aims as expressed in his books, speeches and other documentary evidence before 1939; and (b) the actual measures initiated by Hitler to destroy the Treaty of Versailles and expand Germany's frontiers. Some sort of balanced assessment should then be possible. Good answers will probably show knowledge of the historiographical controversy surrounding the origins of the Second World War.

18 Examine the historiographical controversy over German foreign policy between 1933 and 1939.

This essay clearly requires not a description of Hitler's foreign policy, but an informed discussion of the historiographical debate as conducted by British historians like Bullock, Taylor, Trevor Roper and Irving, and more recent German historians.

19 Examine the view that 'Pragmatism and ideology were in continual opposition with each other during the administration of Hitler's European Empire after 1940'.

Answers must show a knowledge of Nazi policies in occupied Europe, both their origins and implementation. Issues raised will almost certainly include policies towards the Jews and other racial outcasts, the treatment of slave labour, and economic exploitation. Did political and military considerations come into conflict? How systematic, ideologically motivated or opportunistic were these policies?

20 'It is impossible for the historian to be objective in his treatment of the Third Reich.' Discuss this view in relation to your knowledge of the historiography of the period.

Generalised answers on the impossibility of historical objectivity per se or the difficulty of dispassionate analysis of modern history will not earn much credit. Students attempting this assignment must have a knowledge of the historiography of the Third Reich, preferably a combination of contemporary, recent, German and non-German writings. There are several examples of 'controversial' approaches to provide material for the confident student.

Specimen Essay Answer

(*See page 95*)

The answer below is not a model answer, nor does it necessarily represent the only approach. Nevertheless, it is an answer which focuses on the question and does represent the type of answer which may be written under examination conditions, in about 45 minutes.

Assess the respective roles of demagogic leadership and terror in the Nazi political system.

Historians have frequently differed in their assessment of the factors upon which the Nazi political system was based. Alan Bullock, for example, emphasised the demagogic aspect of Hitler's rule, writing that his power 'despite the Gestapo and the concentration camps, was founded on popular support to a degree which few people cared, or still care to admit.' In contrast, Neumann emphasised the terror rather more, labelling it one of the essential principles of Nazi social organisation: Nazi ideology forced compliance through terror, in contrast to democratic ideologies which sought to persuade. Yet even Neumann recognised the charismatic aspect of the Führer-State. The two aspects are not necessarily incompatible, since violence can simultaneously attract and terrorise.

The Nazis themselves did not hold entirely consistent views on the subject. They certainly liked to think that their power rested upon popular support. Nevertheless, they also placed a premium on terror as a means of combatting enemies of the regime and inducing at least outward conformity amongst those Germans described as 'non-Nazi' – those who were neither active supporters nor active opponents of the regime, and who one day might be won over by Goebbels' propaganda. To aid in their campaign, the shadow of the concentration camp was used to good effect, with rumours about them being deliberately fostered by the Gestapo. The United States' prosecution at Nuremberg later stated that 'the deterrent effect of the concentration camps upon the public was a carefully planned thing. To heighten the atmosphere of terror, these camps were shrouded in secrecy.'

Hitler always appreciated the art of the demagogue. There is a penetrating analysis in *Mein Kampf* of the technique of mass suggestion, which can make an action initiated from above appear as the spontaneous activity of the masses. Yet he seems to have genuinely believed that his political system rested upon popular support. In a speech at Hamburg on 20 March 1936 he asserted, 'In Germany bayonets do not terrorise a people. Here a government is supported by the confidence of the entire people. . . In fifteen years I have slowly worked my way up together with this movement. From the people I have grown up, in the people I have remained, to the people I return.' This was more than mere rhetoric – it was an integral part of Hitler's self-belief to assert that he was an incarnation of the will of the *volk*; and yet the cynical Goebbels believed that the most brilliant propaganda had to be reinforced with violence to ensure its effectiveness.

It is not easy to assess the true attitude of the majority of Germans towards Hitler because of the manipulation of public opinion. The Nazis did not win an overall majority in Reichstag elections, but won apparently convincing approval in the early plebiscites. In November 1933 over 95 per cent of the electorate approved of Germany's withdrawal from the League of Nations and the Disarmament Conference; in August 1934 nearly 90 per cent approved of Hitler's action in uniting the offices of President and Chancellor. Thomas Mann correctly predicted the result of the first plebiscite when writing from exile: 'Unhappy, isolated, confused people, seduced by wild and stupid adventurers whom they take for mythical heroes.' The results of the plebiscites, however, may be attributed to genuine feelings of gratitude towards Hitler for supposedly saving the German State, plus the effects of constant intimidation and persuasion, exemplified in a radio address on voting procedure by a State Secretary in the Ministry of the Interior which began, 'The voter goes into the voting booth with ballot and envelope, marks the ballot by placing a cross in the "Yes" circle, puts the ballot in the envelope. . .'

Soon there were few opportunities for public opinion to be expressed. Reports by the Nazis' own security and police services and by opponents indicate levels of dissatisfaction with Nazi policies, but such expressions were rarely directed at Hitler personally. Allen showed in his study of one German town that demagogy played little part in securing Hitler's victory in the first place, and subsequently did not keep him in power. Rather, it was Nazi enthusiasm and initiative at the local level which did most to win support. For some months after January 1933 local enthusiasm was whipped up by demonstrations, marches and propaganda through the media, often aimed at youth, to convince people that a real revolution had taken place. The 'Red Bogey' was used to justify measures against real or imagined opponents, and a general feeling of unease prevailed. Allen concluded that, in the mind of most of the predominantly middle class inhabitants, by 1935 'the bad outweighed the good. Given the chance, they probably would have voted to end or to alter the Nazi regime. But long before 1935 the decision had been cast.'

In other areas terror was certainly more important in encouraging docility. For example, it is difficult to believe that the large working class population of Mannheim saw Hitler as its saviour, or was taken in by propaganda about the nobility of labour, since various left-wing resistance organisations were active there throughout the Third Reich. Gestapo reports in several areas refer to opposition or simply widespread pessimism and ill-humour, kept within bounds only by fear.

Demagogy played a more significant role within the Nazi movement itself than in the political system as a whole. An SA leader declared that the Party's power to attract 'is not due to organisers, but solely to the password "Hitler", which holds everything together.' The fact that Röhm was one of the few Nazi leaders immune to Hitler's magic was doubtless one more reason for his liquidation.

Melita Maschmann and other young converts have described the factors which attracted them into the Nazi youth movement. In her case, the search for a fundamental purpose in life was transferred to Hitler as a personification of the national community, and therefore Hitler was above criticism even when she became disillusioned by the sordid realities of labour service and colonisation activities in Poland.

Coercion played an increasingly significant role in the Third Reich, particularly when the tide of war turned against the Nazis. Yet legal safeguards had already been progressively eroded, and the undisciplined rowdiness of the SA gave way to the more systematic terror of the SS. The centralisation of the police apparatus put even the Party under surveillance, and the police became an instrument of Hitler's personal will, rather than a normal part of the State administration.

It might indeed be argued that the increasing use of coercion showed that the Nazis had failed to achieve a stable social equilibrium, founded upon a genuine identity between leader and followers, and submerging internal differences for the sake of imperialist expansion. Demagogic leadership alone could not achieve this. If the Nazis failed to win over the minds of many Germans, the German nation was ultimately united only in a negative sense, by fear and eventual ruin.

BIBLIOGRAPHY

There are extensive bibliographies on all aspects of the Third Reich in many specialist books. The few titles listed below are all useful, reasonably accessible to students and teachers, and mostly available in paperback.

W. Allen: *The Nazi Seizure of Power* (Penguin 1989). Originally published in the early 1960s, this work is still probably unique in concentrating not on national events but charting the experiences of a single German town, showing how the Nazis won support and then how the townspeople fared under Nazi rule.

K. Bracher: *The German Dictatorship: The Origins, Structure And Consequences Of National Socialism* (Penguin 1973). One of a number of detailed studies of the Third Reich by the post-war generation of German historians.

J. Fest: *The Face Of The Third Reich* (Penguin 1979). This remains a valuable study in which the author assesses Hitler, Goebbels, Göring, Bormann and several other leading Nazi figures, and in so doing considers many of the issues raised by a study of the Third Reich.

J. Fest: *Hitler* (Penguin 1977). One of many useful and readable biographies of Hitler.

R. Grunberger: *A Social History Of The Third Reich* (Penguin 1979). A comprehensive survey not just of social history, but also covers several political and economic aspects.

I. Kershaw: *The 'Hitler Myth'* (OUP 1989). An interesting analysis of Hitler's role in the Third Reich, particularly the part played by the Führer in Nazi propaganda.

D. Peukert: *Inside Nazi Germany* (Penguin 1989). A valuable survey by a German author of the lives and attitudes of Germans during the Third Reich.

E. M. Robertson (Ed.): *The Origins Of The Second World War* (Macmillan 1971). A survey of some of the controversies surrounding Hitler's intentions in foreign policy.

D. Williamson: *The Third Reich* (Longman Seminar Studies 1982). A long and useful introduction surveys many of the issues and debates concerning Germany's domestic history and foreign policy between 1933 and 1945.

ACKNOWLEDGEMENTS

The publishers wish to thank the following for their permission to reproduce copyright illustrations:

Institute of Contemporary History and Wiener Library: pp 27, 28, 29, 37, 41, 48, 57, 58, 59, 61; The Trustees of the Imperial War Museum: pp 30, 32, 33, 34, 35, 36.

The publishers would like to thank the following for permission to reproduce material in this volume:

Hamish Hamilton Ltd for the extract from *The Origins of the Second World War* by A. J. P. Taylor (1964); Odham Press Ltd for the extract from *Hitler – A Study in Tyranny* by A. Bullock (1962); Penguin Books Ltd for five extracts from *The Nazi Seizure of Power* by W. Allen (1984) copyright © William Sheridan Allen, 1965, 1984; Unwin Hyman, part of Harper Collins Publishers for the extract from *The Third Reich* by K. Hildebrand; Weidenfeld & Nicolson Limited for the extracts from *Hitlers Table Talk* edited by Hugh Trevor-Roper (1988) and *The Face of the Third Reich* by J. Fest (1972).

Every effort has been made to trace and acknowledge ownership of copyright. The publishers will be glad to make suitable arrangements with any copyright holders whom it has not been possible to contact.

INDEX